# Praise for THIS IS LEAN

KT-131-295

"*This Is Lean* gives an easily accessible, structured, and inspiring account and description of lean. Most important perhaps is the value and effect of the joint development of the whole organisation, and the structured way of working from co-workers to executives. Here are enormous benefits to gain — both for co-workers, for the company and organisation, and not the least for the customer!"

**HANNA BRANDT GONZÁLEZ**
Permanent Secretary, Unionen (largest union in Sweden)

"*This Is Lean* is much more than a catchy title to another book on lean. It is a lean exploration of a particular operations strategy of fundamental importance to organisations who aspire to add value for those who wish to receive value. It captures the values, principles, methods, and tools which shape a dynamic view of the improvement imperative. And, it does so with resource efficiency – in fewer pages than comparable books – and also with flow efficiency – focusing on the needs of the reader to understand.

Modig and Åhlström have great respect for their reader, with whom they engage as a fellow team member. They tell stories, use metaphors, and sketch scenarios in order to visualise key concepts and to challenge misconceptions. They have great respect for the history of the Toyota Production System and they demonstrate the value of that respect in realising a lean operations strategy. By the end, they leave the reader in no doubt as to their shared understanding of fishing (how to think about improvement) while, at the same time, leaving sufficient actionable space for the reader to figure out his or her own way to learn to fish."

**PROFESSOR PAUL COUGHLAN**
Trinity College Dublin

"The Swedish Social Insurance Agency, which is responsible for the administration of nearly half of Sweden's annual budget, is gradually introducing lean into its operations. Parts of the organisation are in the introductory phases of that process, and other parts are well underway. Regardless of where they are in the process, the book *This Is Lean* plays an important role in guiding our collaborators in understanding lean. In so doing, the book greatly influences one of the major players in the Swedish social welfare system."

**DAN ELIASSON**
Director-General, The Swedish Social Insurance Agency

"*This Is Lean* is a wonderful and original book that will do much to help people gain an accurate understanding of lean management. It presents ideas and concepts in unique ways that are easy for anyone to understand and apply. It is a fantastic book. I absolutely love it."

PROFESSOR BOB EMILIANI
Central Connecticut State University

"For me, lean is about continuous learning! Regardless of whether I have won or lost, I have always tried to learn something new. *This Is Lean* describes why Toyota has become one of the world's most successful organisations. Toyota has always had a constant focus on learning. The ability to learn is *the thing* that creates sustainable success."

MAGDALENA FORSBERG
Biathlon Legend, Inspirational Speaker, Advisor

"*This Is Lean* describes how organisations can develop world-class operational excellence. It is about teamwork, respect, challenging yourself and your team, and continuous improvement. It does not matter if it is an organisation or a top-athlete: the keys to success are universal. World-class performance is a matter of always having the right mind-set!"

PETER "FOPPA" FORSBERG
Ice Hockey Legend, Investor

"Lean is an apparently easy term to remember, but a rather difficult concept to understand accurately. Many executives worldwide still think the real essence of lean production is cost-cutting, which is wrong. *This Is Lean* is one of the most concise, easy-to-grasp, and fun-to-read books on the topic and it will help you understand the essence of this important management philosophy of the 20th and 21st centuries."

PROFESSOR TAKAHIRO FUJIMOTO
University of Tokyo

"This book on Lean Management is a 'must-read' for managers *and* employees, in manufacturing *and* service organisations. Modig and Åhlström have done a great job in not only selecting the most important concepts from the vast literature on lean management but also in providing crystal clear explanations of each concept. Too often management books are padded with interesting but peripheral information, whereas this book doesn't waste a sentence. If your aim is to make your business processes more effective, make sure everyone in your organisation reads this book. Firstly, it will *inform* your employees about lean concepts and, secondly, it will *inspire* them to quickly apply the concepts."

**PROFESSOR KEITH GOFFIN**
Cranfield School of Management

"We apply the thinking described in the book in many functions, including IT and R&D. A common language and methodology facilitates a cross-functional interaction, which is a necessity in a flow-oriented company. The authors have managed to make a complex issue accessible to many people through a logical and clear description."

**PER HALLBERG**
Executive Vice President, Head of Research and Development, Purchasing, Scania

"I found *This Is Lean* most enjoyable – punchy opening, use of some examples/illustrations throughout, good writing style and, most importantly, a sound exposé of the concepts. The book is a most worthwhile contribution to our field."

**PROFESSOR TERRY HILL**
Emeritus Fellow, University of Oxford

"We often turn to the few well-publicised success stories to learn about lean. The truth, however, is that lean continuously evolves as it adapts to any new context it is applied to, so simply copying someone else's recipe rarely leads to a sustainable implementation of lean. In *This Is Lean*, Niklas Modig and Pär Åhlström make an important step forward in transcending past the 'buzz' by illustrating the fundamental mechanisms that are actually at play. It is a truly insightful book that will be of great help to service and manufacturing firms alike in defining and guiding their own lean journey."

**DR MATTHIAS HOLWEG**
Director, Centre for Process Excellence and Innovation
Judge Business School, University of Cambridge

"The best book I have read on lean. It is well written, easy to read, and pedagogical. It is mandatory reading for anyone interested in improving healthcare. Karolinska University Hospital has used the book to train 600 managers."

**BIRGIR JAKOBSSON**
Chief Executive Officer, Karolinska University Hospital

"An easily accessible book that provides the curious with a basic understanding of lean, creates order among concepts for the slightly more initiated and challenges those who think they 'are lean'. This is wonderful reading that I warmly recommend to co-workers, managers, board members, politically elected officials, and all others who want to create more value in what they do."

HANS KARLSSON
Director General, Värmland County Council

"*This Is Lean* is highly applicable reading for executives within all types of industries. It shows that operational excellence is not a static affair but constantly has a need to be reinvented and optimised. High-performing businesses can best sustain their competitive advantage by always forcing a return to a perspective of putting the customer in focus. With too many stakeholders in an organisation pulling in different directions, returning to the essence of the customer experience can be a relief! Lean is a mindset that helps lead the way in these critical iterations. I have not found a book that better teaches the concept and application of lean than this one!"

JOHN LAGERLING
Senior Director, Android Global Partnerships, Google

"The book highlights a phenomenon that is prevalent within the Swedish justice system today. Each area in the justice system is efficient in its own right, but they act independently of each other without coordination, which makes the total system inefficient. An increased focus on flow efficiency within the justice process would create a more humanitarian and faster throughput. The costs for the state would naturally decrease as a consequence."

ANDERS LECKNE
General Manager, Kronoberg Remand Centre

"It is a huge challenge to create a common understanding of lean in a global organisation with operations at 1,600 locations. The book will be of great help in our continuous effort to improve delivered customer value."

CHRISTIAN LEVIN
Executive Vice President, Sales and Services Management, Scania

"The authors have created a simple and logical structure for understanding lean. The book has helped our organisation to focus on the right questions."

HANS NARFSTRÖM
Senior Vice President, Corporate IT, Scania

"The book is incredibly inspiring and targets both 'beginners' and those who already think they know what lean is. My management team and I were so inspired by the book that I decided that all 1,100 employees in my organisation should have their own copy of the book as an inspiration and support in our strategy of becoming a lean organisation. *This Is Lean* has enabled the whole organisation to have a common language around lean, which is a prerequisite for lean to work in a large organisation. The book is easy to read, pedagogically structured, and convincing. I can warmly recommend this book."

ULF NÄSSTRÖM
Vice President, Saab AB, Business Area Electronic Defence Systems

"*This Is Lean* reads like a good novel ... it captures you from the first paragraph (the cancer cases), draws you into the characters (the great concept of flow efficiency), unveils the plot and detail slowly (the laws and theories), before giving away the importance of the relationships (creating and developing lean organisations) and making you feel that all will live happily ever after (just embracing with lean). The examples and explanations in the book are first-class and, having researched and applied lean myself within public services, this book crosses the boundaries in a seamless and relevant manner through focusing on the concepts. It is an imperative read from the beginner to the expert. As with every good book or novel, you learn something new every time you read it!"

PROFESSOR ZOE RADNOR
Cardiff Business School

"Fashion is about self-expression, evoking desirability, and making people dream. Fashion is also, by definition, changing; therefore, flexibility, responsiveness, and rapid time-to-market are core traits of the successful fashion houses of today. *This Is Lean* encapsulates the essence of how well-managed companies create flow throughout the whole value chain and develop a learning capability about what makes their end consumers really happy. Lean is simple, but not easy – for any business leader on a quest of reaching further, while using fewer resources, I can warmly recommend this book."

MIKAEL SCHILLER
Executive Chairman, ACNE Studios

"*This Is Lean* is just fantastic. Really readable, interesting, relevant, and wise. I love the stories – they bring it to life."

PROFESSOR NIGEL SLACK
Emeritus Professor, Warwick Business School

"The world is in a severe crisis. We need to find new ways of managing resources and mitigating the risks of scarcity. *This Is Lean* demonstrates that the current understanding of 'real efficiency' is incorrect. Organisations sub-optimise and waste resources without knowing it. The book captures the latest insights regarding how we have to reform and renew our view on operational excellence. It also shows how holistic thinking, integration, and end-user orientation are the cornerstones of creating both economic and social value."

PETTER STORDALEN
Investor, Hotel Tycoon, Property Developer, and Environmentalist

"*This Is Lean* is a very good introduction to lean thinking and a great help in creating a common picture and language throughout the organisation. First, top management read the book and had a workshop with one of the authors. After that we decided to buy every manager a copy. Now everyone understands our two main principles of 'flow efficiency' and 'securing quality in every step'."

BRITTA WALLGREN
Managing Director, Capio S:t Görans Hospital

"When I read *This Is Lean*, I was very positively surprised. It describes lean in a clear and easy to understand way. We use it extensively in Ericsson and I recommend it to anyone who needs a fast introduction to lean and its benefits."

JOHAN WIBERGH
Executive Vice President and Head of Business Unit Networks, Ericsson

"I have read several books that attempt to explain the true essence of lean throughout my 25 years in automotive business. This is by far the best one. The way it describes lean will be an eye-opener for many people who have  not captured the potential of this complex issue. For everyone managing a value chain today, this book is a must."

LARS WREBO
Senior Vice President, Manufacturing, Volvo Car Corporation

# THIS IS
# LEAN

# THIS IS
# LEAN

## RESOLVING THE
## EFFICIENCY PARADOX

NIKLAS MODIG & PÄR ÅHLSTRÖM

RHEOLOGICA
PUBLISHING

Stockholm 2012

THIS IS LEAN
ISBN 978-91-980393-0-6
First edition

© Niklas Modig and Pär Åhlström, 2012

EDITOR: James Morrison, www.wix.com/jamesedits/jamesedits
GRAPHIC DESIGN AND LAYOUT: Helena Lundin
ILLUSTRATIONS: Helen Bågeryd
COVER DESIGN: Joakim Palm Karlsson and Babak Shermond
PHOTO, COVER: iStockphoto
PHOTO, PORTRAITS OF AUTHORS: Lasse Lychnell (*Niklas Modig*),
Cecilia Nordstrand (*Pär Åhlström*)

PUBLISHER:
Rheologica Publishing
www.rheologica.com

Printed in Sweden by Bulls Graphics AB, Halmstad, 2012

*To Professor Christer Karlsson,*
*who took lean to Sweden.*
*From your first and last SSE PhD.*

# Preface

Years ago, I learned the value of simplifying from a production manager who had stepped into a new position as the head of a large plant. He explained how it allowed him to understand what was going on, as opposed to optimising something that was too complex to understand fully.

This book illustrates the beauty of simplifying. The book cuts through the cacophony of lean terms and methods to the basic ideas and a working definition of lean: a strategy of flow efficiency, with key principles of just-in-time and visual management.

The clarity and simplicity of the concepts allow managers to apply them even in complex operations with many products and many actors, where they easily get distracted by the frequent demands and issues that bombard them. This is valuable for those who do not know what lean is as well as for those who have already studied many lean-associated methods.

*Professor Christoph H. Loch*
*Director, Cambridge Judge Business School*

# Acknowledgements

When we wrote the Swedish version of this book in the summer of 2011, our idea was simply to merge two previously published book chapters. Eight intense weeks later, we had a completely new book. When we had the book translated into English, we decided, for some strange reason, to rewrite it. Perhaps we were adhering to the basic lean principle of continuous improvement. This time, however, we did not spend pleasant summer days in front of our computers, but rather winter and spring evenings and weekends.

But just like last time, we have not done it ourselves. Special thanks go to Sheelagh Gaw, who provided the first translation of the book and all kinds of support in the process of rewriting the translated book. Thanks also to James Morrison, our editor, who helped us polish the language and make it flow. Any remaining oddities are entirely our choice. Thanks to Helen Bågeryd, whose hand-painted illustrations add something extra to the book. Finally, our thanks are owed to Helena Lundin, who had to sacrifice evenings and weekends away from her family to help us transform our text into a proper book, and a very beautiful one at that.

Furthermore, the ideas expressed in this book would not have existed if it weren't for all the organisations we have encountered over the years in our research and through our lectures. You have always opened your doors and met us with enthusiasm. Together, we have been able to develop and refine our ideas of what lean 'is'. Without you, the flow of our knowledge production would be impossible. Many thanks!

We owe our special gratitude to the entities that provided scholarships enabling the study at Toyota in Japan: the European Institute of Japanese Studies, the Japanese Embassy in Sweden, the Japanese Government (Monbukagakusho), Prince Carl Gustaf's Foundation, the Swedish Institute, the Sweden-Japan Foundation, and Doctor of Technology Marcus Wallenberg's Foundation for Education in International Business. Your foresight and generosity in sponsoring exploratory research provided the foundation for this book.

THANKS FROM NIKLAS: I would personally like to thank those people who made it possible to carry out my study of Toyota. Thanks to Takahiro Fujimoto and Tadashi Tanaka, who welcomed me into their research team at the University of Tokyo and who opened the doors to Toyota. Thanks to Ryusuke Kosuge, who is both a close friend and has always been my 'wingman' when researching Toyota. I would also like to thank my family, relatives, friends, and colleagues for all their energy, love, and understanding.

THANKS FROM PÄR: A large and collective thanks to all those who have enabled and participated in my 'lean exploration'. The exploration started in January 1993 with an opportunity to participate in and study the lean transformation of one company. Thank you all for opening your doors to a newly minted PhD student. An important stop on my lean explorations was London Business School, where Professor Christopher A. Voss taught me so much about research and operational excellence.

My warmest thanks go to my family. You are the points of departure and arrival for all my explorations. Thanks to Sheelagh, for her patience, enthusiasm, and constant support. Thanks to Sebastian and Sophie for putting up with my absence: I and my book, well, we are finished now.

FINALLY: Both of us wish to thank our friend, colleague, and mentor, Professor Christer Karlsson, who has not only been a phenomenal supervisor for both of us during our PhD studies, but has also contributed to the conceptual development of lean at a global level.

Stockholm, August 2012

*Niklas Modig*          *Pär Åhlström*

# Contents

PROLOGUE    *500 times faster care*    1

CHAPTER 1    *From resource focus to customer focus*    7

CHAPTER 2    *Processes are central to flow efficiency*    17

CHAPTER 3    *What makes a process flow*    31

CHAPTER 4    *The efficiency paradox*    47

CHAPTER 5    *Once upon a time … How Toyota became number one through customer focus*    67

CHAPTER 6    *Welcome to the Wild West … We call it lean*    75

CHAPTER 7    *What lean is not*    85

CHAPTER 8    *The efficiency matrix*    97

CHAPTER 9    *This is lean!*    117

CHAPTER 10    *Realising a lean operations strategy*    127

CHAPTER 11    *Are you lean? Learn to fish!*    147

EPILOGUE    *Develop a lean outfit!*    155

NOTES    159

# 500 times faster care

## Alison thinks she has cancer

Alison has just discovered a lump in her left breast. A pang of anxiety hits her. She knows that one in ten women develop breast cancer. It is the most common form of cancer among women. Her worry is overwhelming.

First thing Monday morning, Alison decides to find out whether the lump is what she fears. She rings her local doctor's surgery and speaks to the nurse during telephone hours. The nurse is kind and sympathetic and manages to find Alison an appointment for later that day. Alison is relieved and accepts the appointment, even though it isn't with her usual doctor. She calls work and cancels all her meetings for that day.

The doctor is very understanding but cannot ease Alison's worry. He cannot rule out the possibility that the lump could be cancerous. He writes a referral letter that is sent directly to the breast clinic at the local hospital, which will send appointment details to Alison.

Every day that week, Alison checks the mail for the letter from the breast clinic. When a whole week passes without a letter, she starts to get worried. After ten days, she finally rings the breast clinic. She waits in the telephone queue and eventually gets to speak to a nurse. After a five-minute search, the nurse finds Alison's referral letter and promises that they will look into it that day. Four days later, Alison receives a letter from the clinic saying she has been given an appointment for the following week.

On the day of her mammogram and ultrasound, Alison allows herself plenty of time to find parking and the right clinic. Everything goes better than expected, and she is in the waiting room forty-five minutes before her appointment time. She reports to the receptionist, who asks her to sit down and wait her turn.

Alison's appointment time comes and goes, but her name is not called. After five minutes, she asks the receptionist, who says that they are running late and that Alison should just sit down and wait for her name to be called. Fifteen minutes or so after her scheduled appointment time, a nurse comes out and apologises to Alison for making her wait. She is asked to wait in an examination room while the doctor reads up on her case. The examination goes smoothly enough, and Alison is told that she will be sent details of an appointment to see a breast surgeon.

Back at home, Alison talks to her husband about her growing fear. The worst part is not knowing. Her worry even causes her to take time off work.

Ten days after her hospital visit, Alison receives the letter with details of her appointment to see the breast surgeon. Based on the test results, the surgeon cannot be certain that it is cancer, but cannot rule it out either. A second referral is sent, this time to a cytologist, who will take tissue samples for laboratory analysis.

Having received such a vague answer from the breast surgeon, Alison goes home anxious and distraught. She struggles to remember what the surgeon said about the next step. She rings the clinic the next day, but she cannot get through to anyone who can help her. Reluctantly, she leaves her number and waits for her call to be returned.

Someone from the clinic returns Alison's call later that morning and explains about her upcoming visit to the cytologist and the fine-needle biopsy. The clinic has registered her details, and she has been given an appointment in two weeks' time. Alison had been hoping for an appointment within a few days, but the nurse explains that the cytologist is very busy and there are no earlier appointment times available.

When the unpleasant procedure does take place, it goes relatively quickly. The doctor explains that the tissue sample will be sent to the laboratory for analysis and the test results will then be sent back to the breast surgeon Alison met at the breast clinic two weeks earlier. This means that there will be another letter with a new time to meet with the breast surgeon. The nurse is unable to tell Alison how long she will have to wait for the results.

Six weeks to the day after her first visit to her local doctor's surgery, Alison finally gets to meet the breast surgeon again and brings her husband along for moral support. Having read her case file and studied all the test results, the doctor delivers Alison's diagnosis.

## Sarah feels a lump in her breast

While taking a shower on a Tuesday morning, Sarah thinks her left breast feels different, like it has a knot in it. She has a nagging fear for the rest of the morning and cannot concentrate at work.

At lunch, Sarah tells her close friend Susan about her concern. Susan tells Sarah about an article she had read about a trial at the local hospital, the idea of which is to create a 'one-stop breast clinic'. The clinic had been opened a couple of years earlier as a place where women could go without first having to get a referral from their local doctor. Sarah finds out that the clinic is open on Thursday afternoons.

For two days, Sarah is unable to think about anything other than this lump in her breast, which seems to have grown since she first noticed it. Everything she has read on the Internet seems to have made her even more anxious.

Sarah arrives at the clinic shortly before four o'clock on Thursday afternoon. She is immediately greeted by a nurse, who leads her into an examination room and gives her a preliminary examination. The nurse confirms that Sarah's lump needs further examination and Sarah is told to sit in the waiting room while the nurse confers with the breast surgeon.

Fifteen minutes later, the breast surgeon asks Sarah to follow her into the examination room. Sarah is asked to give a brief explanation of why she is there and is then examined by the doctor. The surgeon determines that Sarah will need to undergo a mammogram, ultrasound, and a fine-needle biopsy.

Sarah is sent back out to the waiting room and notices that the other women there look just as worried as she feels. When her name is called out, Sarah follows a specialist nurse into the X-ray room, where the nurse takes pictures of Sarah's breast. A doctor then uses ultrasound to confirm what Sarah already knows: there is a lump in her left breast.

The nurse takes Sarah to a cytologist, who performs the fine-needle biopsy. The doctor cannot say whether it is cancer, but the tissue sample analysis will tell them.

Sarah again finds herself waiting in the waiting room to see the breast surgeon. When she is called in again, she notices that the time is nearly six o'clock. They sit down and the surgeon gives Sarah her diagnosis.

## This is lean

*This Is Lean* is a book about a new form of efficiency that we call 'flow efficiency'. Flow efficiency focuses on the amount of time it takes from identifying a need to satisfying that need. Both Alison and Sarah had the same need: they wanted to find out if they had cancer. They both went through various tests and were given diagnoses. The similarities end there.

From Alison's first visit to her local doctor to the moment she received her diagnosis, forty-two days elapsed, which is equivalent to 1008 hours. In Sarah's case, it only took two hours between her first contact with the nurse at the one-stop breast clinic until she received her diagnosis. Sarah's diagnosis process was more than five hundred times faster than Alison's. Is that a big difference? It is an enormous difference.

The first part of this book (chapters 1–4) defines flow efficiency, how it is created, and why various decisions improve or worsen flow efficiency. In particular, this part explains the efficiency paradox, how and why organisations are actually wasting resources when they think they are being very efficient.

The second part of the book (chapters 5–11) describes how and why Toyota became one of the world's most successful organisations by developing an efficient production flow of cars. Inspired by Toyota, the Western world developed the concept of 'lean'. Today, although lean is one of the world's most widespread management concepts, definitions of the concept are incredibly inconsistent. This inconsistency makes it difficult, if not impossible, to create understanding and form a consensus and, consequently, to succeed with efforts to implement lean. This book describes what lean is, how an organisation becomes lean, and what a lean organisation looks like.

## CHAPTER 1

# From resource focus to customer focus

Alison's and Sarah's stories illustrate two forms of efficiency: resource efficiency and flow efficiency. The traditional and most common of these is resource efficiency. Alison's diagnostic process was carried out in a healthcare system that has been organised to use resources efficiently. Resource efficiency focuses on efficiently using the resources that add value within an organisation. These are the resources that were used in both women's diagnostic process. However, Sarah's diagnostic process was carried out in a healthcare system that focuses on flow efficiency. Flow efficiency focuses on the unit that is processed in the organisation. In both of these cases, the unit is the patients, Alison and Sarah. This chapter examines the two contrasting diagnostic processes in order to illustrate the important differences between resource efficiency and flow efficiency.

## Alison experiences the resource-efficient healthcare system

Alison's healthcare system is organised around a focus on resources and the efficient use of these resources. Her diagnostic process involved numerous organisations and functions – the local doctor's surgery, the breast clinic, the X-ray department, and the cytology department – each of which focuses on a specific area of competence (general medicine, surgery, radiology, and pathology, respectively).

In order for Alison to enter the healthcare system and receive a diagnosis, she needed to interact with the hospital by letter, by telephone, and in person. Alison made a total of five trips, four to the hospital and one to her local doctor's surgery, and had to spend many days contacting the hospital seeking care. She arranged the logistics between these different contacts herself, ensuring that she arrived on time for the appointments. While at these appointments, Alison had to take time off work, with all the costs this entailed for her and her employer.

The time from the first visit to the local doctor's surgery to diagnosis was extremely long compared to the actual time spent conducting the tests of the diagnostic process. The long waiting times between visits created fear and anxiety for Alison. The different steps in the diagnostic process added value for Alison, yet these steps accounted for only a small part of the six weeks between her first and last visits. This point can be seen in the figure on the next page, which illustrates Alison's diagnostic process.

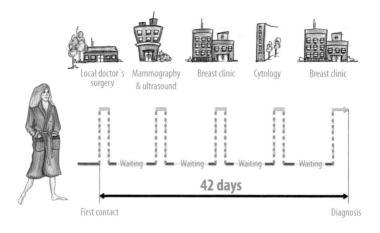

Local doctor's surgery · Mammography & ultrasound · Breast clinic · Cytology · Breast clinic

Waiting — Waiting — Waiting — Waiting

**42 days**

First contact ← → Diagnosis

## Resource efficiency – utilising resources

Resource efficiency, the traditional form of efficiency, involves utilising resources as much as possible. For more than two hundred years, industrial development has been built around increasing the utilisation of resources. A basic principle in this industrial development is to divide an incoming job into smaller tasks, which are carried out by different individuals and organisational functions.

Another principle is to find economies of scale. Grouping smaller tasks together so that individuals, parts of an organisation, or the whole organisation can perform the same task many times over increases resource efficiency. The increase in resource efficiency is often dramatic, with a marked effect on the product's unit cost. Efficient use of resources has long been the most common way of looking at efficiency. It dominates the way in which organisations in different industries and sectors are organised, controlled, and managed.

Resource efficiency focuses on the resources an organisation needs in order to produce a product or deliver a service, such as staff, sites, equipment, tools, and information systems. The organisations that carried out Alison's and Sarah's diagnostic processes employed various physical resources, including buildings, waiting rooms, examination rooms, and X-ray machines, as well as human resources, including nurses, breast surgeons, radiologists, cytologists, nursing assistants, and administrative staff.

Resource efficiency is a measurement of how much a resource is utilised in relation to a specific time period. For example, the measurement can show how much an MRI scanner is used over a twenty-four-hour period:

| | |
|---|---|
| **Resource:** | MRI scanner |
| **Time resource is utilised:** | 6 hours |
| **Time period:** | 24 hours |
| **Resource efficiency:** | 6 hours/24 hours = 25 per cent |

The resource efficiency in this example is twenty-five per cent, which means that the MRI scanner is used for only twenty-five per cent of the actual time period. The time period could also be defined as the X-ray department's open hours, say 8:00 a.m. to 4:00 p.m. In this case, the resource efficiency would be six out of eight hours, or seventy-five per cent.

Of course, resource efficiency is not confined to a single MRI scanner. It can also be measured at a higher abstraction level than individual machines or people. The utilisation of a combination of resources can be measured, for example, for a department or an entire organisation. At an organisational level, resource efficiency indicates how well an organisation is utilising all of its resources and whether the resources are adding value or 'standing still'.

From an economic perspective, it makes sense to strive for the most efficient possible use of resources. The reason for this is the opportunity cost. The following are two examples of opportunity cost:

- If a hospital employs ten doctors, it should make sure that they work as much as possible; otherwise, the hospital could have employed nine doctors and used the money saved elsewhere.
- A hospital has invested tens of thousands of pounds on new X-ray equipment. Consequently, the equipment should be used as much as possible; otherwise, the hospital could have spent part of the money on something else.

Opportunity cost is the loss made by not utilising resources to the fullest. If we have not utilised our resources to maximum capacity, we could have at least used part of the money we used on that resource towards something else. There are many alternative uses for that money, such as paying off a loan, lending money to others, and investing in securities. All organisations face opportunity costs for the money they spend on acquiring or paying for resources, which makes it important for all organisations to use resources efficiently.

In order to understand the importance of resource efficiency, we need only take a look at ourselves. For example, if we buy a new television, it is natural to make sure the television is being used; we want value for money. Therefore, resource efficiency is a natural way of looking at things because it is in our nature to want value for money.

## Sarah experiences the flow-efficient healthcare system

The healthcare system that carried out Sarah's tests consisted of one organisation that focused on a specific patient need: diagnosing breast cancer. The organisation covered a combination of different competence areas. Within the organisation, there was a breast surgeon, a radiologist, a cytologist, a secretary, an X-ray nurse, and an assistant nurse, all within a multifunctional team. Creating an organisation that is organised around a specific need requires all staff to work together.

As a result, Sarah only had to make one visit, during which she met all the specialists in the same place. It took just a few hours of her time, meaning she had to take considerably less time off work than did Alison. Sarah received her diagnosis five hundred times faster than Alison did. The figure below shows Sarah's diagnostic process.

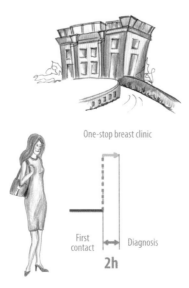

One-stop breast clinic

First contact — Diagnosis

**2h**

## Flow efficiency – satisfying needs

We define flow efficiency as a new form of efficiency. Flow efficiency is new in that it breaks with the historical and natural focus on the efficient utilisation of resources. However, flow efficiency is not an entirely new phenomenon. In fact, the antecedents of a focus on efficient flows can be traced back to the sixteenth century, more precisely, to the Venetian Arsenal in Northern Italy, which was the most powerful and efficient shipbuilding enterprise in the world. The arsenal was capable of producing a fully equipped merchant or naval vessel in less than a day. Elsewhere in Europe, it could take months to produce a vessel of a similar size.

Flow efficiency focuses on 'the unit' processed in an organisation. In manufacturing, the unit is a product comprised of different types of components that are processed in various stages to make the product. In services, the unit is often a customer whose needs are met through different activities. Here, we refer to this form of efficiency as flow efficiency because the focus is on the unit that 'flows' through the organisation: the flow unit. Alison and Sarah are examples of two different flow units that flowed through different healthcare systems.

Flow efficiency is a measurement of how much a flow unit is processed from the time a need is identified to the time it is satisfied. For example, flow efficiency could show how efficiently a local health centre satisfies a patient's need:

| | |
|---|---|
| **Need:** | The patient has a sore throat |
| **Value-adding time:** | Time with doctor and other staff (10 minutes) |
| **Time period:** | Time from the patient's arrival to the patient leaving the health centre (30 minutes) |
| **Flow efficiency:** | 10 minutes/30 minutes = 33 per cent |

The flow efficiency in the table above is thirty-three per cent, which means that the patient receives value during thirty-three per cent of the time she is at the health centre. In this example, it is assumed that the time the patient did *not* spend seeing a doctor or another member of staff (that is, waiting time) does not add value.

Flow efficiency is defined from the perspective of the flow unit, and the important factor is the time during which the flow unit receives value. At an organisational level, flow efficiency indicates how well an organisation processes its flow units. Is the flow unit receiving value or is it 'standing still'?

## Comparing the flow efficiency in two healthcare systems

Alison's and Sarah's experiences illustrate the characteristics and effects of resource efficiency and flow efficiency. The differences are most noticeable when looking at the flow efficiency in the two systems.

Alison's diagnostic process took forty-two days, or 1,008 hours. Assuming that the time involved in the various procedures was two hours, flow efficiency in Alison's case was 0.2 per cent.

*Flow efficiency = 2 hours/1008 hours = 0.2 per cent*

Accordingly, only a small fraction of the entire diagnostic process actually added value for Alison. This shows that her diagnostic process was not flow-efficient.

Sarah received her diagnosis the same day she visited the clinic for the first time, and the time she spent waiting was the actual time it took to analyse the tests. We can assume that Sarah had to wait for a total of forty minutes out of the two hours her diagnostic process took; the remainder of the time she was seeing healthcare staff. This means that the total value-adding time was eighty minutes and, therefore, the flow efficiency was sixty-seven per cent.

*Flow efficiency = 80 minutes / 120 minutes = 67 per cent*

The table below summarises the two examples. The most obvious difference is the time it takes for diagnosis: forty-two days versus two hours. As much as anything, this time difference increased the amount of worry one of the two women felt. The forty-two days of not knowing causes Alison's worry to escalate considerably. Even though Sarah was worried, she spent considerably less time not knowing.

| | Alison's healthcare system | Sarah's healthcare system |
|---|---|---|
| **Total number of contact points and their form** | Several contact points in different forms | One contact through one visit |
| **Time from first contact with healthcare system to diagnosis** | 42 days | 2 hours |
| **Flow efficiency** | 0.2 per cent | 67 per cent |

## Which route to take?

Which is best, resource efficiency or flow efficiency? As we have discussed, resource efficiency is the dominant form of efficiency. As a general rule, organisations are therefore organised around specific functions and specialised around resources. While it is important to use resources efficiently, it is also important to meet customers' needs efficiently. In order to have both high utilisation and satisfied customers, resource efficiency and flow efficiency are both important.

So why would anyone *not* aim to achieve high resource efficiency and high flow efficiency? The answer is that it is very difficult, if not impossible, to score high on both forms of efficiency. We will return to how organisations can combine high resource efficiency and high flow efficiency in chapters 8 and 9.

The best way to understand *why* it is difficult to score high on both forms of efficiency and how it can be done is to understand how processes work. Flow efficiency is created through processes. A process is a collection of activities that, together, create the path for and fulfil the need of a flow unit.

## CHAPTER 2

# Processes are central to flow efficiency

F low efficiency is created through an organisation's processes. In order to understand flow efficiency, it is necessary to understand how processes work. All organisations have processes. There are development processes, purchasing processes, production processes, delivery processes, service processes, and so on. As individuals, we all go through many processes every day. This chapter explains what processes are and describes important elements of processes and flow efficiency. These elements are important because they form the basis for understanding what flow efficiency is.

## Filming Alison's journey towards a diagnosis

In our initial example, Alison went through a diagnostic process that took her from discovering a lump in her breast through to a diagnosis. In order to define Alison's process, we need to take her perspective, which we do by placing an imaginary film camera on her shoulder. This camera records her perspective as she moves forward towards a diagnosis.

By starting filming when she went to the local doctor's surgery and stopping filming when she had her diagnosis, we have defined her process.

Alison's forty-two-day film can be divided into clips that cover the diagnosis and those that do not cover the diagnosis. Examples of clips that cover the diagnosis include Alison's meeting the breast surgeon, the cytologist's taking tissue samples, and the nurse's conducting the mammogram. Examples of clips that do not cover the diagnosis include Alison's waiting at home or travelling to and from her various appointments.

The forty-two-day film can also be divided based on whether the clips added value to Alison. The clips covering activities that did add value to Alison would be labelled 'value-added clips', while those that did not add any value to Alison would be labelled 'non-value-added clips'. Flow efficiency is about deleting all the non-value-added clips then taking all the value-added clips and editing them into a short action movie.

## Processes are defined from the flow unit's perspective

Just as Alison's process was defined based on the film shot by the camera on her shoulder, any process must be defined from the perspective of the flow unit. Flow units are critical in processes as they are being processed. In fact, the word *process*, which comes from the Latin words *processus* and *procedere*, means 'to move forward'. In a process, something is moved forward; we call these flow units. A flow unit can be material, information, or people:

> *Material:* At a car plant, material is moved forwards and processed by machines and assembled in order to become cars. In the breast cancer example, the tests the women take are moved forward and analysed in order to become test results.

> *Information:* When you apply for planning permission to extend your house, you submit an application to the local planning authority. The application goes through various stages and is sent to different parties. In the breast cancer example, the referral letters are examples of information as flow units.

> *People:* An example of people as flow units is customers in a theme park, who go through a sequence of activities from the time they arrive at the park until they leave. In the breast cancer example, the two patients are flow units.

Defining the process from the perspective of the flow unit is important. Many organisations make the mistake of defining a process from the viewpoint of the organisation and its various functions, which would mean that the camera would be on the doctor's shoulder instead. Although the camera would be filming the same activities as if the camera were on Alison's shoulder, it is not the same thing. In order to understand flow efficiency, it is important always to define the process from the perspective of the flow unit.

## Value is defined from the receiver's side

Taking the perspective of the flow unit enables us to understand a subtle but important difference between resource efficiency and flow efficiency. Although the difference (which has to do with the value transfer between a resource and a flow unit) is a general one, it can be explained by returning to the healthcare example.

Any form of activity in which a healthcare system fulfils the needs of its patients involves a transfer of value. The value transfer takes place between the resources of which the organisation consists and the flow unit being processed. The patient is the receiver of the value transmitted by, for instance, the healthcare staff.

A value transfer occurs when one side (the resources) adds value and the other side (the flow unit) receives value. Consequently, we have the following relationships:

- High resource efficiency means a high percentage of value-adding time in relation to a specific time period. The resources add as much value as possible. The movie from the doctor's camera is full of action.
- High flow efficiency means a high percentage of value-receiving time in relation to the total time. The flow unit picks up as much value as possible. The movie from the patient's camera is full of action.

Resource efficiency focuses on the utilisation of specific resources, while flow efficiency focuses on how a particular flow unit moves through the process. The difference between these two forms of efficiency can be expressed as a difference

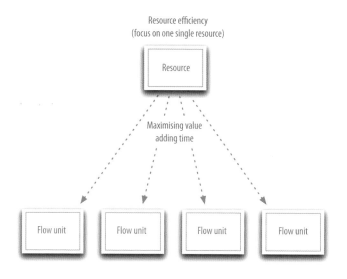

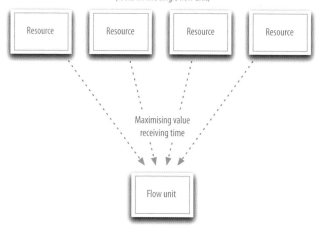

in the dependence between resources and flow units. Is the patient adapting to the situation of the doctor (securing high resource efficiency), or is the doctor adapting to the situation of the patient (securing high flow efficiency)? The figure on the previous page illustrates the difference in dependence for both forms of efficiency. The difference in the dependence is the key factor that differentiates the two forms of efficiency. In resource efficiency it is more important to 'attach work to people' to ensure that each resource always has a flow unit to process. In flow efficiency, however, it is more important to 'attach people to work' that is, to ensure that each flow unit is always being processed by a resource.

## System boundaries define throughput time

An important characteristic of a process is that you can define its start and end points however you want; you determine the *system boundaries*. The breast cancer process could be said to have started when Alison arrived at her local doctor's office and finished when she left the doctor's office. Or it could be said to have started when she first started to worry and finished when she received her diagnosis. You always choose the system boundaries yourself.

It is important where the system boundaries are set, as this determines the critical measure of throughput time. A flow unit's throughput time is one of the elements needed to calculate flow efficiency. Throughput time is simply the time it takes for the flow unit to move through the whole process, as defined, from start to finish.

It is important to look at throughput time from the flow unit's perspective. Alison's throughput time was forty-two days, compared to two hours for Sarah. In these examples, the process was defined as the time from the first contact with the healthcare system to the point at which the patient received a diagnosis.

Most organisations will find it challenging to define a process (and therefore the throughput time) as starting when a need arises and ending when the need is fulfilled. However, it can lead to interesting effects and new innovations. For example, if the throughput time for an airline passenger is defined as starting at the moment the passenger leaves his or her home or office until the time he or she gets on the plane, the throughput time is quite long. For the purposes of shortening this throughput time, the British airline Virgin Atlantic launched a service for busy executives. The service included collecting passengers from their workplace and taking them on a motorbike through the heavy London traffic to Heathrow, where they could take a so-called 'fast track' through the airport. Passengers could board the plane without having to stand in queues and go directly to Upper Class. By seeing the customer's entire flow, Virgin Atlantic was able to offer a service that it could price at a premium level.

## Classifying activities in the process

All processes consist of a sequence of activities in which the flow unit is processed. As in Alison's case, these activities can be divided into various clips or, more generally, different categories. Two underlying dimensions of these categories are particularly important for understanding flow efficiency: value and needs.

### Value-adding activities
The concept of value-adding activities is critical to understanding flow efficiency. It is crucial when defining value-adding activities to take the flow unit's perspective. From the

perspective of the flow unit, activities add value when the flow unit receives value. Value is added when something happens to the flow unit, or when it is moved forward (being processed). Examples of value-adding activities include:

- When materials for a car are processed in a machine;
- When an employee at the local planning authority deals with a planning application; and
- When Alison and Sarah meet healthcare personnel.

Thus, a value-adding activity is one in which the flow unit is being processed. Using the same reasoning, an activity that does not add value – a wasteful activity – is one that does not process the flow unit. Some examples of wasteful activities occur:

- When materials are waiting in a warehouse;
- When a planning application sits in a pile of papers on someone's desk waiting to be dealt with; and
- When Alison is made to wait two weeks for the first available mammogram appointment.

However, it is important to note that even waiting times can add value in certain cases. Maturing cheese or aging whisky are examples of waiting (storage) that add value because the waiting is a part of the process. In these cases, storage adds value to the flow unit (the cheese or the whisky).

### The need defines value

Value is always defined from the customer's perspective. Of course, the concept of 'customer' can be problematic. Who is the customer of the public sector? Who is the customer of the fire brigade? If it is difficult to identify a specific customer, then the focus can shift towards the need that the organisation meets. Instead, we could ask: 'What need does the fire brigade meet?' Among other things, the fire brigade specialises in meeting the need to extinguish fires. Therefore, the process could be defined from the time at which the need is identified (someone discovers a fire) to the point at which the need is met (the fire brigade successfully extinguishes the fire).

### Direct and indirect needs

When people are flow units, it is important to be clear about the difference between direct need and indirect need. Alison and Sarah both needed to find out whether they had cancer. Because this need was the reason the two women started the diagnostic process, we call it a *direct need*. Alison and Sarah also had *indirect needs*, such as the need to feel safe, the need to be met professionally, and the need to understand and be informed. Direct needs are about creating a concrete outcome (for example, reaching a diagnosis), while indirect needs are about the experience.

Therefore, when people are flow units, it is important to look at direct and indirect needs, even though the main focus is often on direct needs. In a hospital accident and emergency department, it is natural to focus on direct needs (saving a patient's life) because the patient can be unconscious or badly injured. On the other hand, if a doctor is giving a patient the results of a cancer test, there will naturally be a strong focus on indirect needs. The doctor will want to ensure that despite having sometimes to break bad news, he or she does so sensitively and creates an experience that is as positive as possible.

In business, strategic choices determine what needs are put in focus. Low-price airlines, for example, focus on direct needs, namely 'transporting individuals'. A customer who buys a business-class plane ticket expects the flight to be a pleasant experience. In that case, both the direct need (the transport) and indirect need (the experience) are met.

Disney's theme parks are great examples of dealing with indirect needs. While we stand in the queue for the roller coaster, things are happening all the time. This makes us feel that we are experiencing value despite the fact we are doing nothing other than waiting. How we perceive what is happening is often more important than what is actually happening (or not happening in this case). The need we have when visiting a Disney theme park is not just to be amused by the attractions (direct need), but also to be entertained the entire time (indirect need).

Upplands Motor, a Stockholm car dealer, is another example of how a company can be good at dealing with customers' indirect needs. Customers entering the dealership are met with the following notice:

> 'Welcome! Please take a ticket and wait your turn. If you wait more than ten minutes from the time you took your ticket to the time you receive help from the service centre, we will give you a free tank of petrol for the car you brought in.'

The wait is never boring at Upplands Motor. They provide their customers with breakfast, lunch, free Internet access, beauty treatments, massages, or a lift to a nearby driving range. Upplands Motor continually focuses on the customer's experience.

## Flow efficiency is value-adding activity in relation to the throughput time

Having defined throughput time and value-adding activities, we can provide a precise definition of flow efficiency:

> *Flow efficiency is the sum of value-adding activities in relation to the throughput time.*

Throughput time in itself is often an indicator of value; that is, the quicker it goes, the better it is. But it does not have to be, as the concept of indirect needs can explain.

Imagine a very flow-efficient dentist. You arrive at the exact time of your appointment. As soon as you get through the door, you are into the practice. There is no waiting room. The chair is already half reclined to save time. You sit down and are recumbent straight away. The dentist is already prepared and so is the drill, which is in your teeth within five seconds of sitting down. The whole procedure is over within five minutes.

This is world-class flow efficiency! Or maybe not. Perhaps the customer has indirect needs. For someone who is afraid of the dentist, this would not be a flow-efficient dentist visit. Such a patient needs time to sit and relax in the waiting room and perhaps go to the loo. The patient wants the dentist to chat and explain what is going to happen. More than anaesthesia, the patient wants reassurance. While all of these activities would add to the throughput time, they would also add value, so the process would be more flow-efficient.

The concept of indirect needs can also be used to analyse the initial breast cancer example. In Sarah's case, she may have received her diagnosis a little too quickly. To go from the first meeting with a nurse to receiving a diagnosis two hours later could be an emotionally tumultuous experience. Sarah may have needed a little more time between the various stages to absorb everything that was happening to her. This is an indirect need that arises from the direct need of a diagnosis. The need always dictates what value-adding activities are and therefore what flow efficiency is.

It is important to clarify that our definition of flow efficiency looks at the *density* of the value transfer from a resource to a flow unit. More specifically, flow efficiency concerns the *share* of the value-adding activities in relation to the throughput time. However, it is also possible to improve customer value by increasing (or decreasing) the *speed* of the value transfer. We will illustrate this with an example.

It is summer, and you want a new look. You make a reservation with your favourite hairdresser, Jean-Pierre at Toni & Guy. He cuts your hair in forty minutes, and the total visit takes fifty minutes. Therefore, the value-adding time is forty minutes out of a total throughput time of fifty minutes, which represents a flow efficiency of eighty per cent.

Your friend is impressed with your new look and books an appointment with Stuart at the Vidal Sassoon studio, who always delivers excellent haircuts. It takes Stuart only thirty minutes to complete the haircut, out of a total time of forty minutes that your friend spent at the salon. Therefore, the flow efficiency of your friend's haircut is seventy-five per cent.

Stuart delivers the haircut ten minutes faster than Jean-Pierre; the speed of value transfer was faster. However, comparing the two from a flow efficiency perspective would indicate that Jean-Pierre is more efficient than Stuart. This is a misleading comparison, though, since the speeds of the value transfer were different. We are comparing apples and pears.

Flow efficiency is not about increasing the speed of value-adding activities. It is about maximising the density of the value transfer and eliminating non-value-adding activities. When it comes to the value-adding activities, flow efficiency emphasises identifying the 'right' speed. What is right for the customer? What is right for the employee? The intention is to maximise quality by striking a good balance.

## Processes are the building blocks of an organisation

There are many misunderstandings about processes. Perhaps the most salient one is that processes are restricted to formalised work routines. Nothing could be further from the truth.

In many organisations, the word *process* is used to describe formalised work routines. These work routines are documented in different systems and describe how a certain task is to be carried out, such as recruiting a new staff member or buying work gloves. Viewing processes only as formalised work routines misses the significance of the term *process*.

If we take our definition of process as a starting point, it should be clear that all organisations have processes, regardless of whether they are formalised. Processes are the cornerstones of all organisations; these are where organisations do what they do. It is through processes that flow efficiency is created.

So how many processes make up an organisation? Some researchers have claimed that all organisations can be described with fewer than twenty main processes, such as from a customer order to delivery or from an idea to a product. That is one extreme. The other extreme can be illustrated using Volvo Car Corporation, which at one time had defined and documented thousands of processes. So which end of the spectrum is right? The answer is that it depends.

The number of processes in an organisation depends first of all on how the system boundaries have been defined, where the organisation sees the process starting and finishing. The organisation can set the system boundaries wherever it wants, which makes it difficult to specify the number of processes.

The number of processes also depends on the level of abstraction. A process at a high level of abstraction can involve different companies that purchase, produce, and sell a product in a supply chain from the raw materials to the final customer. A process at a low level of abstraction can be comprised of the different machines that are used in a factory to produce a single component for a product.

Abstraction levels mean that an organisation can be seen as being made up of a few main processes, each of which is made up of various sub-processes. Every sub-process, in turn, is made up of more sub-processes, and so on. Finally, we arrive at the level of the sequences of individual activities, which are the smallest parts of a process.

Because processes can be defined in different ways and looked at on different levels of abstraction, saying how many processes make up an organisation will always be a subjective evaluation.

CHAPTER 3

# What makes
# a process flow

In order to understand what prevents organisations from having efficient flows, it is important to realise that processes operate according to certain laws. The word 'laws' is vital here. These laws, which can be mathematically proven, are universal; they apply regardless of which type of flow unit is being processed or how the process is defined. This chapter explains three laws, each of which illustrates how processes work and explains why it is difficult to achieve high flow efficiency. The three laws also help us understand why it is difficult to combine high resource efficiency and high flow efficiency. What makes it particularly difficult is that all processes, to varying degrees, are subject to variation.

## The process of boarding a flight

You are late getting to the airport. It doesn't feel good, as you
like to allow yourself plenty of time to browse in the shops and
perhaps choose a new perfume or a bottle of wine. Things have
gone wrong today, right from the moment you left. The taxi
was late due to traffic, which meant you missed the airport
train you had planned on catching.

Luckily, check-in is usually not a problem. Queues have
decreased dramatically since online check-in was introduced.
Fortunately, you have checked in online and secured one of
the much-sought-after emergency exit-row seats, which give
you some extra leg room. Unfortunately, the queue to check-
in has been replaced by a queue for the baggage drop, and, as
there is only one counter open, you just have to join the queue.

Waiting to drop your baggage is more stressful than usual,
as you know the most difficult part, getting through security
control, is still to come. After all the terror attacks that have
taken place all over the world in the last decade or so, security
controls and the associated queues have become the airport's
greatest stress factor.

Passing easily through the automated boarding card check
point, you finally get to security control. As usual, there are
long queues. You look at your watch and realise that time is
getting tight. Your stress levels start to rise, and the only thing
you can think about is getting through the security checks as
quickly as possible. Once through security, it is quite a long
walk to the gate.

You notice that one of the queues is shorter than the others.
Before anyone else has a chance to make the same discovery,
you move to the shorter line. You breathe out and immediately
start to feel a little calmer.

To your dismay, you quickly realise that this queue is actually moving slower than the other one, very slowly in fact. Your feeling of calm turns back to stress. The cause of the delay is an elderly gentleman. He has lots of things he needs to put on the conveyor belt and was clearly not aware that he needs to empty his pockets. He is also told to take off his shoes. He isn't happy, and neither is the security staff. You look across and notice that the lady who was behind you in the previous queue has now passed through security.

*This is not my day*, you think to yourself. You have abandoned the idea of being able to browse in the shops, and you are now preparing to run to the gate.

While running to the gate, you vow that you will leave home much earlier next time; it would be worth it to avoid all that stress. You console yourself with the fact that the sign for your flight has just begun flashing, 'Go to Gate'. You know that you are normally asked to go to the gate a while before boarding commences.

You arrive at the gate just as the final call is announced. You breeze through the boarding and identity card check. But the queuing continues on board, while you wait for everyone to find places to store their hand luggage in all possible and impossible sizes and sit down. Finally, you are seated in your exit-row window seat and you can relax.

Getting from the airport entrance to your seat on the plane can involve a great deal of stress, some of which can be explained with the laws that dictate how all processes work.

## Little's Law

The first law that helps us to understand how processes work is Little's Law. The law is intuitively simple, and we can use the experience of choosing a queue at security control as an example. Little's Law explains why the new queue took longer than the one you first chose.

### Little's Law at security control

Your interest lay in getting through security control as quickly as possible. In other words, you wanted a short throughput time, so you chose the shortest queue. What you did not take into account was the average time it took the staff to check each person. This took longer in the queue you switched to than it did in the queue you initially chose. Throughput time is the product of the total number of people in the queue and the average time it takes to check one person.

The experience of choosing a queue at security control illustrates Little's Law, which states that:

*Throughput time* $=$ *flow units in process* $\times$ *cycle time*

As defined earlier, throughput time is dependent on the system boundaries we have set, that is, where we have decided the process starts and finishes. In this example, the process starts when you join the queue and finishes once you have passed through security control. The system boundaries could also have been defined from the moment you stepped into the airport until the time you stepped onto the plane. What is important is that the laws apply regardless of where we set the boundaries. We must adapt how we define flow units in process, as well as cycle time, to how we have defined the system boundaries of the process.

'Flow units in process' are all the flow units within the chosen system boundaries: all the flow units that have begun the process but have not yet exited it. In the airport example, the flow units in process are the passengers who are standing in the security control queue but have not yet completed their checks.

Cycle time is the average time between two flow units's completing the process and refers to the pace at which flow units move through the process. In our example, the cycle time is the average time it takes between one person's finishing their security checks and the next person's finishing their checks.

The following example shows how you could have applied Little's Law when choosing a queue. Assume that there are fifteen people in the first queue and the queue you change to has ten people in it. In the first, quicker queue, one person passes through security every minute. In the other, slower queue, one person passes through every two minutes. The following would apply:

*Throughput time in first queue* $= 15\,people \times 1\,minute = 15\,minutes$

*Throughput time in second queue* $= 10\,people \times 2\,minutes = 20\,minutes$

*Little's Law and throughput time*

Little's Law shows us that throughput time is affected by two things: the number of flow units in process and the cycle time. A longer cycle time means a longer throughput time. A long cycle time occurs when it is not possible to work any quicker or when there is insufficient capacity.

Little's Law also shows that throughput time increases if the number of flow units in process is increased. The more people standing in front of us in the security control queue, the longer it takes for everyone to get through (given that the cycle time is constant). Therefore, having flow units in process increases throughput time.

There is a paradox here. To ensure high resource efficiency, we must always utilise our resources to a maximum, preferably to one hundred per cent. In order to do this, there must always be work to do; work can never be finished. This means that we need a buffer of flow units so that we do not risk having to wait for work. It is better that the flow units wait for us to be free than wait for them to come to us.

We can illustrate this with a trained specialist in healthcare. If the focus is on a high utilisation of resources, it is better that patients wait for the specialist, rather than the specialist wait for the patients. The paradox, therefore, is that ensuring a buffer of flow units in order to ensure a maximum utilisation of resources serves to increase throughput time.

Returning to the example from the prologue, we can see the effect of Little's Law. In Alison's case, the healthcare system is organised to cope with various diagnoses and the focus is on resource efficiency. It is important to utilise the various specialist functions, so the queues ensure that specialists do not run out of work. This means that Alison must wait between the various stages in the process of getting a diagnosis. The throughput time is long, and flow efficiency is low.

Sarah, on the other hand, experiences a healthcare system focused on one need: the need to obtain a breast cancer diagnosis. There are fewer 'patients in process' at any given point in time, which means that throughput time is shorter and flow efficiency is higher.

## The law of bottlenecks

The second law that helps us to understand how processes work, as well as what prevents organisations from increasing flow efficiency, is the law of bottlenecks. As the example of getting from the doors of the airport to your coveted window seat illustrated, you seldom move through the airport without encountering obstacles. There are many points on the way through the airport at which queues form. These points are called *bottlenecks*. They are stages in the process in the form of sub-processes or individual activities that, like the neck on a bottle, limit the flow. It is here that a person's flow through the airport, from the time he or she arrives at the airport until he or she is seated on the plane, can be blocked.

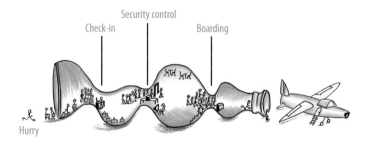

Security control

Check-in            Boarding

Hurry

*Bottlenecks lengthen throughput time*

Basically, the law of bottlenecks states that throughput time in a process is primarily affected by the stage of the process that has the longest cycle time. It is relatively simple to grasp what bottlenecks are, as the airport example illustrates. Formally, a bottleneck is the stage in the process that has the longest cycle time. A bottleneck can also be seen as the stage in the process that has the slowest flow; it is the stage that 'limits' the flow. Consequently, bottlenecks will limit the flow in the entire process.

Processes with bottlenecks have two key characteristics:

1. Immediately prior to a bottleneck, there is always a queue, regardless of whether it is material, information, or people flowing through the process. It is often clear which stage in the process is the bottleneck, particularly when the flow units are material or people. It can be more difficult to see the queue at the bottleneck when the flow unit is information, but the queue is there.

2. The stages of activity after the bottleneck must wait to be activated, which means they will not be fully utilised. Because the bottleneck is the stage of activity that has the slowest throughput, the stages after the bottleneck will work at a slower pace than they could have.

Even if a bottleneck is eliminated, by adding extra resources or working faster, for example, the bottleneck will appear again somewhere else. It is like the arcade game 'Whac-A-Mole', in which moles pop up out of holes and you have to hit them with a mallet to force them underground again. As soon as you hit one (or even before), another one pops up. In the same way, process bottlenecks move and pop up in new places.

Bottlenecks lengthen the throughput time as a queue of flow units form and wait to be processed. This can be understood using Little's Law. As there is a queue, there are flow units in process. Given that we do not change the cycle time (by adding extra resources or working faster), adding flow units in process will increase throughput time.

Because bottlenecks cause delays, it is usually non-value-adding time that lengthens the throughput time. If we strive for high flow efficiency, we will want to avoid bottlenecks in our processes. So, if we strive so industriously to avoid bottlenecks, why do they appear?

*Why bottlenecks appear*

There are two reasons why bottlenecks appear in processes. The first condition for bottlenecks is fulfilled if the stages in the process must be performed in a certain order. In the airport example, you must arrive at the airport before you can drop your baggage. You need to have dropped your baggage before you can pass through security control. You need to have passed through security control before you can go to the gate, and you need to have gone through the gate before you can board the plane.

Of course, it is natural for this condition to be met, particularly if the system boundaries for the process are set relatively wide. The widest possible definition of system boundaries defines the start of a process as the point at which a need has arisen and the end of the process as the point at which the need is fulfilled. Needs cannot usually be fulfilled through activities that can be performed simultaneously in just one place and by the same person. In fact, it is in the nature of an organisation to divide activities that must be performed to fulfil a need into different steps.

The second reason why bottlenecks exist is variation. There needs to be variation in the process. At the airport's security control, people take varying lengths of time to pass through the security control. Some have computers that must be removed from their hand luggage, others forget they have coins in their pockets, and some forget they have perfume bottles larger than the allowed 100 ml. All this leads to variation in service time. In principle, it is impossible to eliminate variation, and it has been shown to have a very negative effect on processes and flow efficiency. This is explained by the law of the effect of variation on processes.

## The law of the effect of variation on processes

The third law that helps us to understand how processes work concerns the connection between variation, resource efficiency, and throughput time. The key here is variation, which has a profound impact on flow efficiency. It has a particularly negative impact on an organisation's ability to combine high resource efficiency and high flow efficiency. For this reason, understanding variation and its impact is central to understanding flow efficiency.

*What is variation?*
There will always be variation in processes. The reasons for variation are potentially endless but can be divided into three different sources: resources, flow units, and external factors.

> *Resources*: Machines may be prone to breakdown, which causes variation. Different doctors take different lengths of time to examine a patient. The layout at the hospital can be confusing, which causes patients to get lost when trying to find the right clinic.

*Flow units:* Customers at a hair salon have different requests for hair-cuts. Cars at a repair workshop have different types of problems. Some planning applications are incorrectly filled out, which means they take longer to process.

*External factors:* Patients' arrival times at the accident and emergency department are not evenly distributed. Sales of chocolate Easter eggs mainly take place at one time of year. Two busloads of hungry students arrive unannounced at a drive-through fast food restaurant.

Regardless of the source of the variation, it affects time: either processing time or arrival time. There will be a variation in the time it takes to process different flow units and/or there will be a variation in the time between different flow units arriving into the process. Some examples will help illustrate:

- In car manufacturing, quality problems can arise in machines, and the company needs to rework a product, leading to variations in processing time.
- Different applications for planning permission take different lengths of time to process. Some people fill in the application forms correctly; others do not. Some have simple requests, while others are more complicated. These differences lead to variations in processing time.
- In the breast cancer example, patients may arrive late for their mammogram appointment, leading to variations in arrival times.
- Demand for the fire brigade's services are seldom evenly distributed over time. It is also difficult to predict when a fire will start, leading to variations in arrival time.

There is a relationship between a variation in processing time and variation in arrival time. In a process made up of different stages, variation in the processing time in one stage will lead to variation in arrival time in the following stage.

As these examples illustrate, it is impossible to imagine a process without variation. Variation is particularly difficult to avoid when the flow unit is a person, as all individuals are unique and have individual needs, especially indirect needs. People introduce a natural variation that is very difficult to avoid. It is not possible to standardise how we deal with people in the same way as we can standardise how we deal with material or, to a certain degree, information. In fact, it is impossible to imagine a process without variation, although the degrees of variation will differ.

*Relationship between variation,*
*resource efficiency, and throughput time*
The major influence that variation has on flow efficiency can be explained by the relationship between variation, resource efficiency, and throughput time. This relationship was formalised in the 1960s by Sir John Kingman in his famous Kingman's Formula and is illustrated in the figure on the next page.

The figure shows how throughput time (on the vertical axis) is dependent on utilisation (on the horizontal axis):

- Throughput time increases the higher we move up the vertical axis.
- Utilisation on the horizontal axis is a measure of how efficiently the resources are utilised. The closer to one hundred per cent, the higher the resource efficiency.

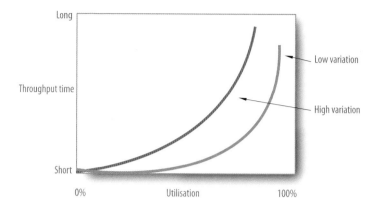

The relationship between throughput time and utilisation is shown in the form of two curves: one for the case of low variation and the other for the case of high variation in the process.

The forms of the curves above show the first effect of variation. The curves show that the closer we get to one hundred per cent utilisation, the longer the throughput time. Increasing utilisation from ninety per cent to ninety-five per cent increases throughput time to a greater degree than increasing utilisation from eighty per cent to eighty-five per cent; this is despite the fact that the increase in both cases is five per cent. In other words, the connection between throughput time and utilisation is exponential rather than linear. This means that the closer we get to one hundred per cent utilisation, the greater the effect an increase in utilisation will have on throughput time.

The other effect of variation can be seen by comparing the two curves in the graph above. The curve showing the case of high variation is moved to the left compared with the curve showing the case of low variation. Assuming that utilisation is constant, this relationship means that:

*The greater the variation in the process is, the longer the throughput time.*

The significance of variation in processes is fundamental for understanding flow efficiency. By way of comparison, if all of the cars on a motorway maintained exactly the same speed, there would be no build-up of traffic. Queues form when, for different reasons, cars do not all drive at the same speed.

## Process laws and flow efficiency

In order to understand what prevents organisations from having high flow efficiency, it is necessary to understand the three laws in this chapter. The laws provide reasons as to why the throughput time in a process increases:

- Little's Law states that throughput time increases when there is an increase in the number of flow units in process and when the cycle time increases.
- The law of bottlenecks states that throughput time increases when there are bottlenecks in the process.
- The law of the effect of variation states that throughput time increases as variation in the process increases and the process gets closer to one hundred per cent resource utilisation.

So what do the laws say about flow efficiency? In chapter 2, we defined flow efficiency as the sum of value-adding activities in relation to the throughput time. If throughput time increases, the general rule is that flow efficiency will decrease. This rule applies if the increase in throughput time is not met by an increase in value-adding time.

For example, imagine that an increased throughput time can be compensated for by creating indirect value for the customer.

Adding value to the wait for an amusement ride, as Disney has done, may avoid having the increase in throughput time negatively affect flow efficiency.

However, the normal situation is that, if the throughput time increases, flow efficiency will be reduced. In other words, the three laws help us understand what causes low flow efficiency: number of flow units in process, cycle time, bottlenecks, variation, and resource efficiency.

The laws also show that it is difficult, if not impossible, to combine high resource efficiency with high flow efficiency. High resource efficiency, particularly if there is variation in the processes, requires flow units' waiting to be processed. The risk of running out of work must be avoided. According to Little's Law, having flow units in process reduces flow efficiency. Furthermore, for a process with high levels of variation, the law of the effects of variation shows that it is impossible to combine high resource efficiency and high flow efficiency.

So how can flow efficiency be improved? With the help of the laws, it is essentially possible to do four things. Of course, doing all of these things is easier said than done, but at a very high level of abstraction, the following activities are what improve flow efficiency:

- Reduce the total number of flow units in process by eliminating the causes for the queues (of material, information, and people). Naturally, the causes will be many and will vary between processes.
- Work faster, which reduces cycle time.
- Add more resources, which increases capacity and reduces cycle time.
- Eliminate, reduce, and manage the different forms of variation in the process.

What makes these activities particularly difficult is the fact that many aspects of organisations are designed to improve resource efficiency. As noted in chapter 1, it is very important to improve resource efficiency. However, as the process laws have illustrated, focusing on and improving resource efficiency increases the chances that flow efficiency will suffer.

Another problem with focusing too closely on resource efficiency is that it risks creating multiple problems and extra work, which can sometimes represent a large proportion of an organisation's total work. Consequently, even if a particular resource has high resource efficiency, the work that 'keeps the resource busy' is not really adding value. We call this the *efficiency paradox*.

## CHAPTER 4

# The efficiency paradox

**M**any organisations are more focused on resource efficiency than on flow efficiency. High capacity utilisation is not only seen as a good thing, it is often the main goal. On this basis, a very well-managed organisation would have no available capacity. Although this may be beneficial from the organisation's point of view, it can represent a problem from a customer perspective. This chapter highlights the downside of focusing too much on resource efficiency and the negative effects of the low flow efficiency that would result. These negative effects create the need for a lot of additional resources, work, and efforts that would not be necessary in a flow-efficient organisation. The paradox is that a greater focus on utilising resources efficiently tends to increase the amount of work there is to do. This chapter explains this efficiency paradox and highlights three sources of inefficiency.

## The first source of inefficiency:
## long throughput times

Highly resource-efficient organisations experience a range of negative effects. These effects are negative not only from a customer perspective, but also from a company and employee perspective. These negative effects emanate from three 'sources of inefficiency'. The first of these is related to *time,* as the following examples illustrate.

*Alison's waiting time generates new needs*
In the example at the beginning of the book, Alison had to wait forty-two days to receive her breast cancer diagnosis. Such long waiting times create dissatisfaction, frustration, and, most importantly, worry. Alison's concern could have been overwhelming, even causing her to take time off work, which may have required her employer to hire a replacement. If the replacement were not as skilled as Alison at this particular job, it would necessitate training. Even with the training, the replacement might not be as productive as Alison and could make mistakes that negatively affect the customers and employees of Alison's company. And so on.

This story shows that non-fulfilment of a need can create new types of needs, which in turn create new needs. In other words, there is a chain reaction. Let us go through the story and illustrate this chain of cause-and-effect.

Alison initially wanted a diagnosis. This is what we call the *primary need* because it is the root cause that led her to initiate the diagnostic process. However, because it took so long for her to go through the diagnostic process (that is, to have her primary need fulfilled), various *secondary needs* developed. Her concern had time to grow, which led her to take time off work. This created another secondary need for her employer to hire and train a replacement. However, despite the training, the replacement made a mistake, which created yet another secondary need to recover an unhappy customer. Therefore, the failure to fulfil Alison's primary need created a chain of cause-and-effect that generated numerous new secondary needs. Although this scenario is hypothetical, the point is that the waiting time triggered new types of needs. The following example further illustrates this chain of cause-and-effect.

*Waiting time closes important windows of opportunity*
Imagine an organisation in which everyone is really busy at the end of the year. This busyness has caused several people to be late for the meeting to decide the location of the next year's winter conference; consequently, the meeting starts fifteen minutes late. Towards the end of the meeting, it emerges that details about one of the potential conference venues are missing because there had simply not been enough time to find the information. This means that the meeting needs to be rescheduled. The attendees pull out their calendars, and, after five minutes of deliberation, an available slot is found for two weeks later. The new meeting is eventually held, and the location for the winter conference is chosen.

When the chair emails the conference centre to confirm the reservation, he receives the following reply: 'We have not heard from you for over two weeks. Unfortunately, the date you have requested is no longer available'. A new meeting is required to discuss whether the location or timing of the event should be changed.

In this example, the primary need is to decide on the location of the winter conference. However, because people were delayed and did not have the time to find all the relevant information, the decision had to be postponed. This led to a number of secondary needs' arising. The delay made it necessary to compare calendars to find a new meeting time, to issue a new meeting invitation, and to have the new meeting. The subsequent unavailability of the conference centre necessitated a new meeting. As in Alison's case, this is a chain of cause-and-effect that generates numerous secondary needs.

*Long throughput time generates secondary needs*
These two examples illustrate the negative effects of things' taking a long time, the underlying problem both for Alison and in choosing the conference centre. In other words, the examples illustrate the negative effects of long throughput time, which, as we saw in chapter 3, is a consequence of overly high resource efficiency.

The core problem in both examples is that the negative effects caused by long throughput time often generate new secondary needs. It is like a game of dominoes: when the first domino is toppled, it knocks over the second one, which knocks over the third one, and so on. Metaphorically, long throughput time is what caused the first domino to topple. It is a source of inefficiency that generates various problems. The figure below illustrates the domino effect caused by Alison's long throughput time.

Long throughput time generally has negative effects on people and often leads to boredom, worry, and frustration. We can lose our drive and inspiration. We can start to forget or find we just don't care. These effects can often generate challenges and

problems that organisations must deal with, which requires
new resources and new activities.

## The second source of inefficiency: many flow units

The second source of inefficiency that appears in a highly
resource-efficient organisation is the need to *handle many things*
at the same time, which is closely related to the first source
of inefficiency. For instance, the longer we wait to answer our
email, the more emails we will have to answer. The longer we
wait to take care of our travel receipts, the more receipts we
will have to take care of. The following illustrates some of the
negative effects of handling many things at the same time.
Again, the core problem is that secondary needs are created.

*Inventory requires additional resources*
A manufacturing company with low flow efficiency will face
increases in inventory, which create several secondary needs.
Firstly, inventory requires storage space, which is costly and
leads to other costs, such as heating, administration, and security. Secondly, large volumes of inventory and work-in-progress
make it more difficult to have a good overview. Without an
overview, a lot of time and effort is spent looking for materials.
Thirdly, inventory and work-in-progress tends to hide problems. Imagine a step in a manufacturing process that starts to
produce a poor-quality component. With a large number of
products' being worked on, it is difficult to find and eliminate
the quality problems. These are examples of having secondary
needs generated because of a large inventory. The key here is
that the secondary needs would not exist if there were less
inventory. The negative effects of inventory are illustrated in
the figure on the next page.

*Too many emails trigger stress*

Email is a wonderful invention, but an inbox with two hundred unsorted emails can be somewhat overwhelming. Where do you start? The primary need is to answer important emails. However, the large number of emails creates a secondary need for a strategy to sort emails. One strategy could be to address the emails in date order, while another could be to start with the most important people first. Or perhaps you could look for 'flagged' messages or discard those emails on which you have only been copied.

Whatever method you use, sorting, structuring, and searching are activities that fulfil the secondary need, which is to handle the large amount of email. The primary need is to read, answer, and store email, but the large number of messages necessitates certain activities in order to gain some kind of overview. Apart from creating unnecessary work, handling a large number of emails at once can also be stressful.

*Juggling with too many things makes people lose control*

When too many things are being handled at the same time, human limitations cause a number of secondary needs. For example, if a service company has to manage many customers at the same time, individual customers may feel like they are just one in the crowd. It is difficult for a restaurant to meet the needs of each customer if there are thirty other customers waiting to be served. Staff will not have a clear overview and may treat customers impersonally. How many times have you dealt with a service organisation and found that the staff hardly acknowledged you? The more customers there are inside the process, the harder it is for each one to feel acknowledged and special, which can create new secondary needs. Making neglected and frustrated customers happy requires extra resources.

In white-collar work, the impact of the human factor is particularly pronounced when there are too many things to handle at the same time, such as on-going projects and cases. Advances in information technology have meant that storing information in itself does not lead to significant costs; however, storage does tend to lead to a poor overview. It is easy to lose sight of the big picture when work is piling up. The human brain is believed to be able to remember approximately seven units at the same time. After this, we start to forget, which is when we make mistakes. In other words, we are not equipped to handle a lot of things at the same time.

*Handling many flow units generates secondary needs*

Regardless of whether it is inventory, emails, or tasks, the above examples show how the need to handle too many things at the same time leads to the creation of new secondary needs. The need to handle many things at the same time is fuelled by a focus on resource efficiency.

We saw in chapter 3 how a focus on resource efficiency means that the number of flow units in process will increase. Regardless of whether it is customers, projects, tasks, products, or materials that are processed in an organisation, there will be many flow units that are being worked on but are not yet finished. This is because it is natural for a resource-efficient organisation to ensure there is always work to do and to avoid running out of work.

There are various negative effects that occur when an organisation or individual has to handle many flow units at the same time. We lose control, which makes us frustrated and stressed. It is difficult to get a good overview, which often means that problems are hidden within the pile of work-in-progress. Handling many flow units at the same time forces an organisation to invest in additional resources and develop structures and routines. These all fulfil secondary needs that only exist because the organisation has to handle a large number of flow units.

## The third source of inefficiency: many restarts per flow unit

The third source of inefficiency created in a highly resource-efficient organisation is a need for many *restarts*. The examples below illustrate what restarts are and why restarts have negative effects on organisations.

*Starting over on the same task generates mental set-up time*

Restarts are created when you have to start over on the same task. An example is managing a large email inbox. There is a high risk that you will need to read messages more than once. Some messages are simply too complex to deal with at that time, so you read them, file them, and return to them later. Sometimes you have to come back to them more than once, perhaps because you need further information.

When work to be done just sits in a pile waiting, it is easy to lose sight of the big picture. The time and energy we spend on categorising and structuring the work creates delays. The delays and the different type of activities (such as searching, identifying, categorising, and structuring) mean that we have to re-familiarise ourselves repeatedly with the same information.

The challenges of starting over on the same task are also driven by mental set-up times. A person needs time to focus his or her mind on a task, and it is mentally challenging to deal with several tasks at the same time. It is particularly challenging when we must repeatedly shift our focus from one task to another. The fewer tasks we have to deal with at the same time, the easier it is to focus. The more frequently we have to switch between tasks, the longer the mental set-up time becomes in relation to the total time.

Therefore, the limitations of the human mind mean that a high number of restarts will generate new secondary needs that would not have been created if the work had been finalised the first time.

*Many handovers generate frustration*

Restarts are also created when different people have to start over on the same task, as the following illustrates. Imagine you are having some problems with your newly purchased mobile phone, so you call your mobile operator. You are greeted by an automated recording that gives you half a dozen options from which to choose. You don't recognise your particular requirement among the options, so you just press a button, only to be given four new options. You press another random button and finally end up waiting for an operator.

You listen to the voice announce, 'You are in a queue and we will help you as soon as possible', without telling you *how* soon. You wait for what seems like hours, but is most likely ten minutes. Eventually, a real person comes on the line, but he cannot help you and has to transfer the call to a colleague. Luckily, the wait for this new person is short as you have bypassed the queue. You recount your problem once again, but, amazingly, a third person is needed to deal with your query. Your frustration increases, and you vent this frustration on the third person.

This example illustrates a type of restart, or handover, which is created when a customer is passed between stages. Your call was switched between different operators, and it took three attempts before you found a person who could help with your query. You had to explain your situation to each operator, which became very frustrating.

The number of handovers is partly driven by the way in which the process is designed. Processes in which each flow unit only meets one resource (machine or person) are possible, but quite rare. Processes are usually designed in such a way that each flow unit has to pass many resources on its way through the process. It is uncommon to find processes in which all of the necessary tasks can be completed in the same place by the same person or machine.

### Many handovers generate defects

Handovers also risk the 'Chinese whispers' effect, whereby the information being passed on becomes more distorted as the number of handovers increases. Many handovers also risk creating a mind-set of, 'Now I am finished with my bit, you go ahead and do your bit'. In such cases, there is no real responsibility for the whole and there are often problems of sub-optimisation. This can lead to the creation of secondary needs in the handover, or the interface between two stages in the process.

### Many restarts generate secondary needs

Regardless of whether an employee starts over on the same task or tasks are handed over between different people in an organisation, the examples illustrate how restarts generate new secondary needs.

Underlying the problem of restarts are the two consequences of focusing on resource efficiency that we dealt with previously: long throughput time and many flow units in process. In a resource-efficient organisation, things take time and many things need to be handled at the same time. These two factors mean that the number of restarts increases.

As the task of processing a flow unit is disrupted by many restarts, various secondary needs will occur. We forget, so we have to rework. We face mental set-up time, which makes us inefficient. Information can be lost, which leads to mistakes. Handovers are done inaccurately, causing problems and duplicated work.

## Secondary needs generate superfluous work

A customer engages with an organisation to satisfy a primary need. If the organisation's flow efficiency is low, however, this can generate secondary needs. As illustrated in this chapter, these secondary needs can be generated from having long throughput times, many flow units in process, and many restarts per flow unit.

The primary need is that of the customer when engaging with the organisation in the first place. Secondary needs can arise as a consequence of a failure to meet the primary need.

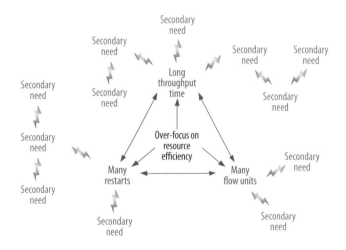

It is important to understand that secondary needs can often generate other secondary needs in a chain reaction, as is illustrated in the figure above. As a consequence of this domino effect, secondary needs can be harmful to organisations. Secondary needs consume resources, even if no 'real' customer value is created.

But what is the root cause of secondary needs? Essentially, an over-focus on resource efficiency creates low flow efficiency.

This creates 'efficient islands' in which fulfilment of customer needs is split up into several, smaller steps that are performed by various individuals or parts of an organisation. No one island has a full overview of the entire process; each island sees only its own part.

In such situations, it is easy to create an organisation in which each part is sub-optimised. Although the individual sub-optimised parts are efficient, the flow efficiency of the whole process will suffer, and there is a risk of creating a series of secondary needs.

Secondary needs are harmful for organisations since they generate what we call *superfluous work*, or work devoted to taking care of secondary needs. Superfluous work is a very sophisticated form of waste, since we often fail to realise that it is waste. We think we are adding value, but we are not.

When a busy nurse answers a call from Alison, who wants to know her status in the queue, the nurse feels she is adding value by answering the question. However, if Alison had received her diagnosis more quickly, she would not have to take up the nurse's time, which the nurse could have spent dealing with waiting patients. Thus, Alison's waiting time created superfluous work for the healthcare system.

## Managing receipts: the art of being extremely inefficient

The authors of this book have gained a better understanding of the nature of superfluous work by reflecting on some of our own practices. Neither of us particularly enjoys managing all the financial paperwork that is generated during the course of a normal month. There are taxi receipts that must be kept for travel expense claims, credit card receipts that need to be checked against the monthly credit card bill, and all kinds of bills. There are receipts for private expenses and receipts for work-related expenses and so on.

At irregular intervals during the month, we empty pockets and wallets full of receipts into a 'receipt box'. As we both are very busy (utilising our capacity to the full), we postpone dealing with the receipts and bills. We wait until it is no longer possible to cope because the pile in the receipt box is making us feel concerned. Perhaps we have missed paying an important bill? This is not to mention the money that is outstanding from not having submitted the expense claims.

So we dive into the pile and try to bring order to it, but the pile is chaotic and receipts are difficult to find. As researchers in the area of managing operations, we begin devising systems to create order.

We buy colourful sorting trays and a label maker to create labels (acts that, ironically, generate even more paperwork). We are then able to carry out the various activities that bring order to our receipts. The first activity is to structure the receipts by date. The second activity is to take all the receipts from a certain day and sort them by credit card. Once this is done we can start to file a particular receipt. Unfortunately, we often forget what the receipt referred to, which means the third activity is to refer back to our calendars and find out what actually generated the receipt. The fourth and final activity is to file and document the receipt. By now, we start to feel pride in the systems we have created and the value we have added.

But is all the work we have put into creating a system for our paperwork really adding value? No. The first three activities are superfluous work. Amidst all the action, superfluous work is correctly perceived as adding a lot of value; we have to take care of all the receipts whether we like it or not. Yet the core of superfluous work is that it addresses a need that has arisen

due to a failure to satisfy the primary need (filing the receipts). The root cause of superfluous work is actually a failure.

Why? Firstly, each receipt has a long throughput time. No value is added from the point at which we receive a receipt until we deal with it. The only thing we do is to empty the receipts in a box. This means that some receipts have to wait over a month to be processed, by which time we have forgotten what the receipt was for.

Secondly, because we waited so long, we had to take care of many receipts, which meant we had to structure and sort them, and search for information on the activity that generated the receipt. We even had to invest in physical resources (the trays and the label maker) in order to be able to structure and sort the receipts.

Thirdly, the processing of each receipt involved at least four restarts since we had to look at each receipt at least three times:

- Structure → What date?
- Sort → What type?
- Searching → What activity generated the receipt?
- Filing and documentation

Many of the activities involved in sorting, structuring, searching, and filing the receipts in our system would not have been
necessary if we had adopted a flow efficiency perspective. Such
a perspective would have meant dealing with each receipt and
bill more or less as soon as it appeared, or at least much more
frequently than we currently do. This would help remove
superfluous work. We would not need to structure and sort
the receipts because we would only have a few receipts to deal
with. We would not even need the colourful sorting trays.

Furthermore, even with our 'great' system, many of the
receipts are so old that we find it difficult to recall what they
refer to, which means we have to spend time trying to remember the nature of different expenses. Sometimes we lose both
the receipt and our memory of it. These are all examples of
superfluous work. The figure below illustrates the relationship
between superfluous work and value-added work.

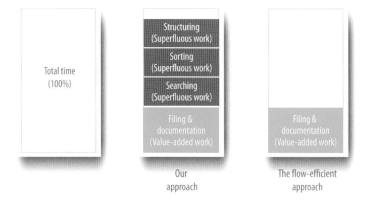

Although this is only a simple example, it is a good illustra-
tion of how organisations work. Much of the work we do in
organisations is also superfluous. The figure above shows that
only a very small proportion of the total time we spend on
our receipts is 'real' value-added work. This often applies in
organisations as well. Answer the following question honestly:

*How much of the time that you spend at work is spent on fulfilling secondary needs? In other words, how much of your total working time is dedicated to superfluous work?*

For us, the answer is 'a lot'.

'But I am really busy, so I must be efficient,' you might argue. Well, the question is whether you are actually creating real value (meeting primary needs) or fulfilling secondary needs.

## The efficiency paradox

Superfluous work is what creates the efficiency paradox. By over-focusing on resource efficiency, process laws guarantee that flow efficiency will suffer. If flow efficiency suffers, then several secondary needs will be generated. Activities to meet these secondary needs may seem like value-adding activities, but they would not be necessary if the primary need were already fulfilled. The paradox is that we believe we are utilising our resources efficiently, but we are actually being inefficient, since much of that utilisation comes from superfluous work and non-value-adding activities, as illustrated in the figure below.

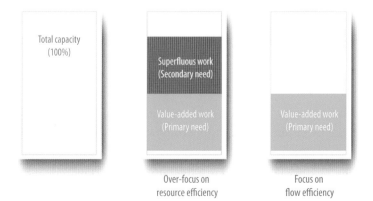

Total capacity
(100%)

Superfluous work
(Secondary need)

Value-added work
(Primary need)

Value-added work
(Primary need)

Over-focus on
resource efficiency

Focus on
flow efficiency

The efficiency paradox exists at an individual level, as illustrated in the example of our sorting receipts. The paradox also exists on an organisational level, as your answer on the question of how much time you spend on superfluous work probably showed. But what if the efficiency paradox also exists at the societal level?

It may be that a lot of the work that keeps our organisations busy is pure waste. People may think they are efficient because they are busy, when they are actually wasting a lot of resources. What does this mean for how we manage resources on a societal level?

## Resolving the efficiency paradox

The efficiency paradox means we are wasting resources at the individual, organisational, and perhaps even societal levels. This begs the question of how we can resolve the paradox?

At the core of resolving the paradox is a focus on flow efficiency. By focusing on flow efficiency, an organisation can eliminate many of the secondary needs that arise as a consequence of low flow efficiency. More specifically, any decision that decreases throughput time, the amount of flow units in process, and/or the amount of restarts will eliminate superfluous work. Paradoxically, *not* focusing on utilising resources makes it possible to free up resources.

The idea is that, by focusing on flow efficiency, flow units should flow quickly through the organisation. In a flow-efficient organisation, there is no need for numerous restarts since there are few flow units in process. In an extreme case, each flow unit will be dealt with as efficiently as possible; nothing will be 'standing still'. Depending on how the process has been designed, flow units may have to be handed over between stages in the process, but these handovers will be smooth and fast. There is a continuous flow, and everyone sees and takes responsibility for the whole process.

The flow-efficient organisation is analogous to a relay race. In a good 4 x 100 metres relay team, the handovers are smooth and all four runners can see what is happening all the time. By the time the first runner has nearly completed the first hundred metres, the second runner has already started running in order to simplify the handover and speed up the race. When the baton is handed over, no time is lost as both runners are at top speed. A case in point was Yohan Blake handing over the baton to Usain Bolt in the final of the 4 x 100 metres at the 2012 London Olympics. The Jamaican team ran the 400 metres in 36.84 seconds, a world record for baton flow efficiency!

In a resource-efficient organisation, however, the first 'runner' is carrying many batons at once. In fact, the more batons the better. But after he has run the first hundred metres, there is no one to meet him. A phone call reveals that the second runner is in Thailand for a meeting. It takes several more calls to find someone who is free to run the second leg. By the time the batons are handed over, nine days later, two have been lost and one has been forgotten. This is not a gold medal-winning formula, but it is, unfortunately, how many organisations behave.

An interesting question then would be, 'How many resources we could avoid wasting if we started to see the "big picture" and focus on flow efficiency on a societal level?' The world's resources, such as food, energy, and water, are in greater demand than at any other time in human history. How much better could our society become at managing our natural resources if we eliminated sub-optimisation and 'island thinking'?

One strategy for resolving the efficiency paradox is a concept called 'lean', which involves focusing on flow and creating organisations that are more like an efficient relay race. It is about seeing the whole in order to avoid island thinking and focusing on real customer needs. Lean has been extremely successful in eliminating waste and superfluous work in many industries, yet the concept is poorly defined and poorly understood. The second part of this book looks more closely at lean. First, however, we need to understand where the term 'lean' comes from.

## CHAPTER 5

# Once upon a time ... How Toyota became number one through customer focus

As we have already seen, focusing too much on resource efficiency has several negative effects. Focusing on flow efficiency is a way of overcoming these negative effects. A company that systematically chose to focus on flow efficiency was Toyota Motor Corporation. This choice laid the foundation for what we now call lean. This chapter will take you through the history of the company and illustrate why Toyota came to focus on flow efficiency and what effect this move had on the evolution of Toyota's production system.

## The history of Toyota Motor Corporation

Kiichiro Toyoda founded Toyota Motor Corporation in 1937 with the idea of producing cars for the local Japanese market. After the Second World War, Japan needed to rebuild its industries. Some representatives of Toyota Motor Corporation travelled abroad, for instance to the United States, seeking ideas for how to set up successful car production. Two things in particular puzzled the Toyota representatives. The first was that there was so much stock and the second was that so many products needed to be repaired at the end of the production line. These two factors stood in stark contrast to the Toyota representatives' own views.

Kiichiro's father, Sakichi Toyoda, had developed some basic principles that would later prove very important for Toyota's car production. In 1896, Sakichi had launched an automated loom that would revolutionise the textile industry. The loom had a function that was unique at the time: textile production stopped automatically when a thread broke. This made it immediately possible to identify, analyse, and eliminate the problem that had arisen. The concept was later termed *jidoka*, which means, 'automation with a human touch'. Machines developed 'human intelligence' in the sense that they could identify a problem automatically. Jidoka became the core of Sakichi's philosophy and later became one of the two pillars upon which Toyota built its production system.

When Kiichiro established Toyota Motor Corporation, he took his father's philosophy from the textile industry as a starting point, by 'finding the thread' throughout the entire production process. This led to the development of *just-in-time*, the second pillar upon which Toyota's production system was based. Just-in-time is about creating flow in production by eliminating all inventory and only producing what the customer wants. Every single product should 'flow' through the production system.

## Toyota faces an economy in crisis

To understand why Toyota focused on flow efficiency, it is important to understand the problems that faced Japan immediately after the Second World War. The country's scarce resources at the time had a huge influence on how the company developed. Toyota faced what Professor Takahiro Fujimoto at the University of Tokyo calls 'economies of scarcity'. The following resources were particularly scarce:

- *Land.* Japan is a small nation in which land is a scarce resource.
- *Technology and machines.* Japan's industrial development lagged behind that of the Western world, particularly the United States.
- *Raw materials.* There was a shortage of iron and steel due to high transport costs.
- *Financial resources.* Japan was a country in crisis and remained so for many years after the war. No financial institutions could finance the expansion of the motor industry.

Faced with this lack of resources, Toyota had to develop a new way of thinking about efficiency. The answer was to focus on flow efficiency. The development of Toyota's production system came to be characterised by several important factors.

## Focus on doing the right things

The first effect of the resource scarcity was that it increased the importance of 'doing the right things', which meant providing the product that the customer wanted. Because Toyota lacked capital, there was an intent focus on investing in the right technology and the right materials. The company could not risk making a bad investment and had to ensure that its product offering was what customers actually wanted. Accordingly, Toyota used build-to-order production: nothing was produced that had not been ordered.

To produce only what had been ordered, Toyota learned the importance of really knowing customers' needs. Customer needs were broken down into three questions:

- What (which product) does the customer want?
- When does the customer want the product?
- What amount does the customer want?

The first question dealt with *what* potential car-buyers needed and desired. Establishing close customer contact enabled Toyota to understand fully what customers needed, which meant the company could develop products with the desired design and function. Once the product had been developed, Toyota chose to invest in relatively simple machines with a low level of functionality. The machines focused on producing exactly what Japanese customers wanted.

To avoid the risk of producing cars that were not sold, it also became important to know *when* and *how many* cars to produce. Toyota developed a so-called 'pull system', which meant that a car was not produced until there was an actual customer order. When a customer ordered a car, the relevant order information was sent upstream in the production flow, through the entire production system. The information answered the questions of what, when, and how many the customer wanted.

The key to the pull system was that Toyota saw the whole production process as one flow made up of different production steps. Every step had two roles: internal supplier and internal customer (see the figure below).

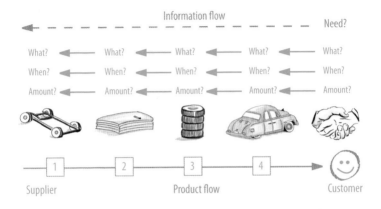

The figure shows a simplified version of the production process comprising four steps, where the fourth step is closest to the customer. In step four, the customer order is taken and the need is identified: what, when, and how many. The customer's need is then broken down by asking the following questions:

- What (components/materials) do I (step four) need to satisfy the needs of the external customer?
- When do I (step four) need these (components/materials) to be able to produce and deliver the finished product to the external customer at the promised time?
- How many (components/materials) do I (step four) need to be able to produce the product?

According to the breakdown in the figure, step four becomes the internal customer of step three. Step three, in turn, becomes the internal customer of step two, which becomes the internal customer of step one. In this way, the needs of the external customer are broken down and the information concerning the order is spread upstream through the entire production process. Step one will then place an order for the requisite materials with an external supplier. Production can then begin, which is done by each step's delivering its part to the next step in the production process.

In this example, it is not just the external customer's needs that are clearly defined and communicated. All parts of the production process must define and communicate what, when, and how many units they need. In this way, value is constantly added to the product as it flows downstream through the production process. Material is pulled through the production process, from purchasing to delivery of the finished product. This means that no inventory of the product is created. Everyone knows what to do, everyone knows when it has to be done, and everyone knows the correct number of units required.

## Focus on doing things right

The second effect of having scarce resources was to 'do things right' by efficiently processing the produced goods to avoid having too much capital tied up in work-in-progress or finished goods inventory. Toyota strived for a quick transformation of the product, from the purchased raw materials to the delivered and paid-for final product.

In order to achieve the pull system, Toyota mapped out the entire production process. The needs of external customers were the trigger in a long chain of value-adding activities.

With this customer-orientated view, Toyota's goal was to maximise flow through the process: a fast information flow in one direction and a fast product flow in the other. Toyota wanted to avoid having work-in-progress between the steps in the production process and strived to eliminate anything that could inhibit the flow through the process. All forms of inefficiency or waste that did not add value to the product were eliminated to improve flow.

Toyota identified seven forms of waste that inhibited the production flow and did not add any value, either to the product or the customer:

- *Waste of overproduction.* Each step in the production process should always produce only what the customer needs.
- *Waste of time on hand (waiting).* Production should be organised to avoid all unnecessary waiting, both for machines and workers.
- *Waste in transportation.* Avoid transporting material and products, by changing the layout of the factory.
- *Waste of processing itself.* Avoid doing more work on a part or a product than the customer requires; this includes using tools that are more precise, complex, or expensive than necessary.
- *Waste of inventory.* Inventory represents capital that is tied up in the process and hides problems; it should be avoided by means such as reducing machines' set-up times (the time it takes to change a machine from doing one thing to doing another).
- *Waste of movement.* Organise the workplace so that workers do not need to move in order to do things such as gathering material or fetching tools.
- *Waste of making defective products.* Every step in the production process is responsible for producing only fault-free parts.

Toyota's focus on doing things right meant that the company avoided the risk of delivering an incorrect or faulty product to the customer. Quality assurance and control became very important. Every Toyota employee was made responsible for quality to ensure that products were right from the start. Jidoka was adapted to car production by running a cord along the ceiling over the production line, which anyone could pull to stop production when a problem occurred. Problems were seen as opportunities for development and improvement. Problems were something positive that should immediately be identified, analysed, and eliminated, never to reoccur. A mistake should never reach the customer.

## The economies of scarcity created a strong focus on seeing the whole

The most important point in the Toyota story is that the lack of resources forced the company to develop a production system that focused on flow efficiency. The resource scarcity forced Toyota to focus on customers' needs. Toyota saw all steps in the production process as internal customers and suppliers, which created an understanding of the big picture. All parts of the production process were links in the same chain.

The company communicated customer orders upstream in the flow through the entire process so that the requested product could be pulled downstream. The goal was to maximise flow efficiency so that value was added to the product one hundred per cent of the throughput time, from order through to delivery and payment. The production process was flow-efficient. It was Toyota's production process that Western observers termed 'lean'.

## CHAPTER 6

# Welcome to the Wild West ... We call it lean

Toyota's internal production philosophy, the Toyota Production System (TPS), has been developed over nearly a century. Today, TPS is a well-known concept in the West and a role model for manufacturing and service organisations alike. TPS is even more fully established in Japan. Development in Japan has gone so far that virtually every bookshop in the country sells books such as *TPS for Dummies* and *Let's Study TPS in English*. Towards the end of the 1980s, there was a surge of interest in Toyota among Western researchers. They assigned the label 'lean' to their observations, thereby launching a new concept. Although the term 'lean' was created with Toyota as a starting point, lean and TPS are two different concepts. Although they have been developed and described in parallel, they are two different concepts.

## Ohno defines the Toyota Production System

Taiichi Ohno started his career within the Toyoda family's group of companies in 1932 and is often referred to as 'the Father of TPS'. Through common sense and total dedication to the company over nearly sixty years, Ohno continuously developed Toyota's production philosophy. Together with Eiji Toyoda, cousin of Kiichiro Toyoda, the founder of Toyota, Ohno gave the philosophy the name 'Toyota Production System'. In 1978, Ohno published a book entitled *Toyota Production System: Beyond Large-Scale Production*. Ohno rejected economies of scale and large-scale production and maintained that productivity was created through flow:

> 'All we are doing is looking at the time-line from the moment the customer gives us an order to the point when we collect the cash. And we are reducing the time-line by reducing the non-value adding wastes.'

Initially, Ohno's book was published only in Japanese. It remains the most read book among Toyota's Japanese employees and is referred to as the company's bible. Although the book is aimed at manufacturing, Toyota's managers claim that everything that any leader needs to know about TPS can be read 'between the lines' of the book.

Ohno's book was first published in English in 1988. Prior to its publication, many Western authors had tried to explain TPS, but none had managed to do so in an easily accessible way.

## Lean sees the light of day

The term 'lean production' first appeared in 1988, when it was used by John Krafcik in his article 'Triumph of the Lean

Production System', published in *Sloan Management Review*. The article compared productivity levels between different car manufacturers and identified two types of production systems: a robust system and a fragile system. Krafcik destroyed the myth that productivity was created through economies of scale and advanced technology (robust production systems) and proved instead that those factories (such as Toyota's) that had low inventory, low buffers, and simple technology (fragile production systems) were able to deliver high productivity and high quality. Krafcik thought that the term 'fragile' had negative connotations; instead, he used the term 'lean' to represent the efficient production system.

## The book that changed the world

The ideas that Krafcik's article expressed were developed as part of the International Motor Vehicle Program, in which Krafcik participated. The research programme was housed at MIT in Cambridge, Massachusetts, and included leading researchers from all over the world. In 1990, based on this research, the international best-selling book *The Machine that Changed the World* was published. The authors, James P. Womack, Daniel T. Jones, and Daniel Roos, provided a comprehensive view of what lean production was about. The book was the result of many years of research and showed how Toyota successfully managed to achieve productivity and quality levels that none of its competitors could. The book argued that lean is made up of four core principles:

1. Teamwork
2. Communication
3. Efficient use of resources and elimination of waste
4. Continuous improvement

Womack and Jones have since continued to develop the lean concept and have published many articles and books. In 1996, their book *Lean Thinking* focused on what a company should do in order to 'be lean'. The book outlined five new principles with a clear focus on implementation:

1. Specify value from the standpoint of the end customer.
2. Identify the value stream and eliminate all steps that do not add value.
3. Make the remaining value-creating steps flow, so that the product flows smoothly towards the customer.
4. When the flow is established, let the customer pull value upstream from the next upstream activity.
5. When steps 1 through 4 are complete, the process starts all over again and continues until a state of perfection is reached in which perfect value is created with no waste.

By applying these principles, a company could start to 'leanify' its operations and improve the flow in its processes. *The Machine that Changed the World* and *Lean Thinking* have both been worldwide best-sellers and have made the greatest contributions to developing and spreading the lean concept.

## Fujimoto places focus on Toyota's capabilities

Relatively few books about Toyota were published during the 1990s. A notable exception is Takahiro Fujimoto, who in 1999 released *The Evolution of a Manufacturing System at Toyota,* a book that attracted a lot of attention in Japan. Fujimoto gave a historical account of the evolution of Toyota's production system and managed to capture many abstract phenomena. Fujimoto argues that Toyota has developed three different levels of capabilities:

- Level one – routinised manufacturing capability
- Level two – routinised learning capability (Kaizen capability)
- Level three – evolutionary capability (capability-building capability)

In particular, Fujimoto argues that the key to Toyota's success is the capability of always ensuring development, regardless of what setbacks or obstacles the company encounters.

## Decoding Toyota's DNA

At the same time as Fujimoto launched his book, researchers Steven Spear and H. Kent Bowen published an article in the *Harvard Business Review* entitled, 'Decoding the DNA of the Toyota Production System'. This article again brought TPS to the attention of the Western world. The article was based on a longer study of Toyota's production system in which the authors tried to decode the tacit knowledge absorbed within TPS. The results were presented as four rules for designing, operating, and improving processes and the activities in the processes:

1. All work shall be highly specified in terms of content, sequence, timing, and outcome.
2. Every customer-supplier connection must be direct, and there must be an unambiguous *yes* or *no* way to send requests and receive responses.
3. The pathway for every product and service must be simple and direct.
4. Any improvement must be made in accordance with the scientific method, under the guidance of a teacher, at the lowest possible level in the organisation.

This article has become one of the most frequently quoted articles on the topic. It is one of the few sources that manage to illustrate in a clear and simple way just how Toyota thinks about its organisational improvements.

## The Toyota Way is encoded internally by Toyota

In 2001, Toyota released an internal publication called, *The Toyota Way*. This document, which outlined Toyota's core values, was translated into various languages and distributed throughout the Toyota Corporation to promote a consensus view within the multinational company. *The Toyota Way* comprises five basic values that are categorised within two key areas: *continuous improvement* and *respect for people*.

**Continuous Improvement:**

- Challenge – We form a long-term vision and meet challenges with courage and creativity to realise our dreams.
- *Kaizen* – We continuously improve our business operations, always striving for innovation and evolution.
- *Genchi Genbutsu* – We practice *genchi genbutsu;* we go to the source to find the facts to make correct decisions, build consensus, and achieve goals at our best speed.

**Respect for people:**

- Respect – We respect others, make every effort to understand each other, take responsibility, and do our best to build mutual trust.
- Teamwork – We stimulate personal and professional growth, share the opportunities of development, and maximise individual and team performance.

*The Toyota Way* is only sixteen pages long, and each value is illustrated with a testimonial from a Toyota employee. The publication has never been made officially available outside of Toyota and is still only used internally as a manual for Toyota's production philosophy. *The Toyota Way* represents the company's core values.

## Liker launches The Toyota Way

In the early 2000s, books on Toyota and TPS were not high on the best-seller lists in Western countries. This changed when Toyota became the world's largest car manufacturer. Around this time, in 2004, Jeffrey K. Liker published a book that he also entitled *The Toyota Way*. This book has become very popular, not only in the manufacturing industry, but also in the service industry. The book outlines Liker's own interpretation of Toyota's philosophy based on his many years of experience studying Toyota in the United States. He packages his version of *The Toyota Way* in the form of fourteen principles:

### I. Long-term philosophy

1. Base your management decisions on a long-term philosophy, even at the expense of short-term financial goals.

### II. The right process will produce the right results

2. Create a continuous process flow to bring problems to the surface.
3. Use 'pull' systems to avoid overproduction.
4. Level out the workload.
5. Stop the process if necessary to fix problems in order to get the quality right the first time.
6. Standardise tasks and processes for continuous improvement and for employee empowerment.
7. Use visual control so that no problems are hidden.
8. Use only reliable, thoroughly tested technology that serves your people and processes.

### III. Develop your people and your partners

9. Grow leaders who thoroughly understand the work, live the philosophy, and teach it to others.
10. Develop exceptional people and teams that follow the company's philosophy.
11. Respect your partners and suppliers by challenging them and helping them improve.

### IV. Continuously solve root problems to drive organisational learning

12. Go and see with your own eyes in order to understand the situation thoroughly.
13. Make decisions slowly by consensus, and implement decisions rapidly.
14. Become a learning organisation through relentless reflection and continuous improvement.

## Lean explosion!

Lean has continued to develop in parallel with the release of the books on TPS. Both academics and practitioners have developed lean into a concept in its own right that is separate from the writings on Toyota, even if it is still largely associated with the Japanese car giant.

Although lean originally developed within the manufacturing industry, the concept has been adapted to other functions, environments, and industries, including such functions as purchasing, product development, logistics, service, sales, and accounting. The concept has also been adapted to other industries, such as banking and insurance, retail, consulting, media and entertainment, healthcare, medicine, telecom, and IT.

The interest in Toyota and lean has led to hundreds of books and articles. A quick search on Amazon for business books released in 2011 with the word 'lean' in the title revealed over one hundred different titles. A summary of the usages of the term 'lean' in the subject matter of the books is found below:

| | | |
|---|---|---|
| Lean accounting | Lean IT | Lean revolution |
| Lean acres | Lean labour | Lean selling |
| Lean agile | Lean leadership | Lean service |
| Lean and green | Lean library | Lean six sigma |
| Lean banking | Lean manufacturing | Lean software |
| Lean business schools | Lean management | Lean start-up |
| Lean culture | Lean marketing | Lean supply chain |
| Lean design | Lean ministry | Lean sustainability |
| Lean doctors | Lean office | Lean system engineers |
| Lean education | Lean problem solving | Lean transformation |
| Lean enterprise | Lean product development | Lean thinking company |
| Lean healthcare | Lean publishing | Lean training games |
| Lean hospitals | Lean R&D | |

A lean explosion just hit the world! Suddenly, it seems as though everything has become lean. Suddenly, this is lean, that is lean, and this is lean too! With so many books available, it is difficult to distinguish between what lean *is* and what lean *is not*. Some books deal with lean as an abstract concept, like an approach, a philosophy, a culture, or as principles. Other books treat lean as something more concrete: a way of working, a method, tools, and techniques. There is no single generally accepted definition of lean. This fragmentation presents a problem for practitioners and academics alike because this constantly developing concept refers to different things.

CHAPTER 7

# What lean is not

There are as many definitions of lean as there are authors to define it. Many of these definitions have developed lives of their own outside of Toyota. Even the writings about Toyota are many and varied. While there is a lot to learn from all this literature, it is remarkable that there are so many inconsistent definitions of lean. This chapter discusses three problems with the various definitions of lean. Firstly, the definitions are made at different levels of abstraction. Secondly, lean has become a means instead of an end. Thirdly, lean seems to have become all that is good, and all that is good is lean.

## Problem 1: Lean is defined
## at different levels of abstraction

Do you want a piece of fruit, a pear, or a green apple? It is
difficult to answer this question accurately because the three
alternative answers are not on the same level of abstraction.
Fruit is at the highest level of abstraction because it encom-
passes all three possible answers. Because the pear is a fruit and
can be defined by the type of fruit (pear), it is on the second
level of abstraction. The green apple is a level lower again,
because it is defined not only by the type of fruit (apple), but
also its colour (green). The higher the level of abstraction, the
more general the definition. The lower the abstraction level,
the more specific the definition. 'I want a piece of fruit' is a
more general statement than 'I want a green apple'. The figure
below illustrates the problem of different levels of abstraction.

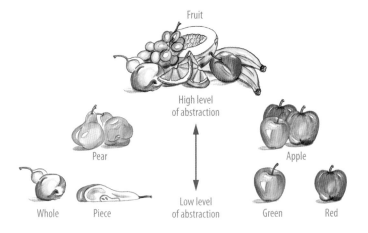

*Lean is everything from fruit to green apples*
The literature on lean freely mixes the levels of abstraction and
treats lean as everything from fruit to green apples. Such con-
fusion also occurs in practice, as illustrated in a questionnaire

survey we conducted. The survey was answered by sixty-three people, all with extensive experience working with lean in fourteen different industries. The first question was, 'What is lean?' The answers could be divided into seventeen different categories, or definitions, of lean:

| | | |
|---|---|---|
| Way of working | Quality system | System for understanding |
| Philosophy | Way of life | Mind set |
| Approach to improvement | Method | Values |
| Approach | Production system | Management system |
| Systems thinking | Strategy | Toolbox |
| Culture | Elimination of waste | |

The fact that there are so many definitions is a clear sign that, in practice, lean is defined at different levels of abstraction. In order to sort these definitions into different levels of abstraction, it is necessary to differentiate between:

- Fruit level (lean as a philosophy, culture, values, way of living, way of thinking, etc.)
- Pear level (lean as a way to improve, quality system, production system, etc.)
- Green apple level (lean as a method, tool, elimination of waste, etc.)

*Lean as green apples*
Most of the writers who have defined lean have done so at the level of green apples, that is, at a low level of abstraction. Of course, the underlying principles have been presented and described many times, but the overwhelming focus of most authors is on the methods and tools Toyota developed. Because what we observe is concrete and easy to understand, it is natural

to describe the methods and tools. We can observe what Toyota does and describe its methods. We can observe what Toyota has and describe the tools its employees use.

Some have gone so far as to choose just one of the methods Toyota developed and equate that to lean:

'Implement this method and your company will be lean!'

Others have focused on identifying and describing all the tools that Toyota has developed. They present an entire lean 'toolbox':

'Use this package of tools and your company will be lean!'

The problem with defining lean simply as methods and tools is that lean tends to become specific to a certain type of context or environment. Toyota developed its methods and tools within the large-scale manufacturing of cars. This resulted in the designing of tools and methods for that specific context and environment and not necessarily for other contexts. This, in turn, runs the risk of limiting the applicability of the methods and tools.

If lean is defined at a low level of abstraction, an organisation risks misunderstanding what lean is about. This limits the concept's application areas.

### Service industries grow pears as if they were apples

Defining lean at the level of green apples, or as the methods and tools that Toyota has developed, limits the applicability of lean when it is taken into other industries or sectors of society. In the last ten years or so, service organisations have become interested in using lean to improve efficiency. As a result, the concept is starting to be relatively widespread in both the private and public sectors.

Many organisations start their lean journey using the methods and tools that Toyota developed. However, this means that they risk losing the deeper thinking around lean and tend to ignore the *why* behind the use of the tools. Fully understanding the depth of lean takes a long time and is more abstract than just methods and tools. It is much easier to start with something concrete.

Many organisations are very good at adapting and modifying the tools and methods to their specific service environments, in which there are high demands on flexibility and variation. Other organisations have abandoned lean because they found it difficult to make these adaptations. When faced with these difficulties, the organisation generally reacts sceptically to lean. For example:

> 'We work with people at a hospital, not with cars. We don't mass-produce patients.'

> 'Our services are too customer-orientated and specific to certain situations for us to standardise our way of working.'

Reactions like these lead to organisations' concluding that lean is not for them. They do not see how the methods and tools can be useful in their environment.

If lean has been presented to an organisation as 'green apples'; that is, something that is specific to a manufacturing process, then such reactions are unsurprising. The more context-specifically a concept is defined, the narrower its area of use. Knowledge about how to grow a delicious and beautiful green apple is not necessarily of value for growing a delicious and beautiful pear. Knowledge about how products are produced efficiently is not necessarily valuable for the efficient delivery of services.

In summary, there are a few important consequences of defining lean at different levels of abstraction. The higher the level of abstraction at which lean is defined, the more general the definition. The lower the level of abstraction at which lean is defined, the more specific the definition. Furthermore, it means that the higher the level of abstraction, the wider the area of use, and the lower the level of abstraction, the narrower the area of use. By defining lean at a low level of abstraction, it is not necessary that the methods and tools will be suitable outside the particular environment in which they were developed. Defining lean at the wrong level of abstraction creates a high risk that it will be abandoned.

## Problem 2: Lean as a means instead of an end

When the Swedish athlete Carolina Klüft retired in 2008, she reigned supreme as the queen of the heptathlon; she had never been beaten as a senior heptathlete. Between July 2001 and September 2007, she won three World Championship titles, one Olympic gold medal and two European Championships.

Klüft has often said that the reason behind her success is that she thinks competing is 'fun'. She has always emphasised her continual enjoyment in competing. Klüft emphasises the state that she wants to reach – a goal – instead of focusing on the means she uses to achieve that goal.

In sport, it is common to direct focus on the means:

'Use this golf club and you will hit the ball as far as X …'

'Eat Y and you will be able to run faster …'

'Rest as much as Z and you will avoid injury …'

The means describes *how* and the goal describes *why*. The problem with focusing on the means instead of the goal is that the connection between the means and the goal is not the same for everyone; the same means do not necessarily always lead to the same goal. Just because someone has the same equipment as Carolina Klüft and trains the same way, this does not automatically mean they will necessarily have fun. The focus on the goal creates flexibility, whereas a focus on the means may create limitations.

The same problem has arisen in the conceptual development of lean. The means and goal have become confused with one another. There has been a strong focus on *how* Toyota works by emphasising and defining its values, principles, methods, and tools. They are different means for creating some sort of change, or means to achieve a goal. Unfortunately, a problem arises when the focus falls on 'which means' Toyota uses, rather than asking and understanding 'why' these means were used, that is to say, the goal behind Toyota's philosophy.

If lean is defined as methods, the use of these methods tends to become a goal in itself. For example, a method that is often used at Toyota is standardisation. Problems arise when that method becomes the goal and not a means of achieving a goal. One goal of standardisation is that it provides a foundation for continuous improvement. In order to improve, the company must create a common ground from which it can improve; otherwise, there is nothing to improve.

Confusing means and goals often causes an organisation to overlook *why* it is going through a change process. Instead, the organisation places too much importance on the specific means being used. When asked whether the organisation works with lean, the proud answer is:

'Yes, of course! All our departments have now put up a visualisation board, and we gather around it every morning for a
meeting.'

The means have become the goal. The organisation sees itself
as 'lean' just because it successfully implemented a specific tool
or specific method. The goal behind the implementation of
the tool or method is lost. Why, then, is a visualisation board
necessary?

Unfortunately, the strong association between these methods and Toyota has led to the goal of thinking and acting more
like Toyota. It is important to remember that what Toyota does
is linked to its environment. Again, knowing how to grow a
delicious and beautiful green apple is not necessarily useful
when you want to grow a delicious and beautiful pear.

## Problem 3: Lean is everything that is good and everything good is lean

If the means and the goal are confused with one another, what
goal do organisations then have in their work with lean? The
questionnaire survey mentioned earlier in this chapter asked:
'Why did your organisation implement lean?' The sixty-three
respondents provided as many as forty-five different reasons:

| | |
|---|---|
| Create a common approach | Free up time |
| Create a common way of working | Improve cash flow |
| Create a culture | Improve cleanliness |
| Create a learning organisation | Improve collaboration |
| Create a standardised way of working | Improve commitment |
| Create a universal solution | Improve competitiveness |
| Create commitment among managers | Improve control |

| | |
|---|---|
| Create continuous improvements | Improve customer satisfaction |
| Create efficient collaboration | Improve delivery precision |
| Create respect for the individual | Improve emplooyee satisfaction |
| Create responsibility at the individual level | Improve flexibility |
| Create stability | Improve growth |
| Create stimulating work | Improve information transfer |
| Create teamwork | Improve leadership |
| Crete long-term strategy | Improve motivation |
| Decrease costs | Improve production |
| Decrease delivery times | Improve productivity |
| Decrease inventory | Improve profitability |
| Decrease lead times | Improve quality |
| Decrease mistakes and problems | Improve sales |
| Decrease waste | Improve service |
| Develop employees | Improve work environment |
| Develop leaders | |

Which organisation would not want to achieve all of those goals? The answers indicate every conceivable positive result, regardless of the type of organisation. This response is not uncommon. Researchers and practitioners alike often see lean as the solution to all problems. But if lean is the answer to all problems, then what is lean *not*? If lean is everything that is good, and everything good is lean, what is the alternative? If lean solves all our problems, do we need anything else?

In order to add to knowledge, researchers develop theory. Theory is an attempt to explain and predict the world around us. To be useful, however, theories must be constructed in such a way that they can be proven wrong. If there are no alternatives, the theory will become trivial. The way lean is defined by both academics and practitioners prevents it from being falsified. For example, who wouldn't subscribe to the list of benefits stated above?

The problem with current definitions of lean, as with many of the conclusions we draw regarding how successful organisations run their businesses, is that they are trivial. This implies that the knowledge does not add any value because it is obvious. For example, imagine if a detective was asked whether she knew anything about a murderer and answered:

> 'We have worked out that the murderer is a person. This person has a head and a heart, and needs to eat and drink regularly to survive.'

These conclusions are trivial because they are obvious. They do not add any value to the investigation, and they cannot rule out any suspects. The conclusions are not falsifiable. The chances of apprehending the suspect are not increased. If the answer changed, the value could also change:

> 'The murderer is a man. He has shoulder-length hair with a centre parting and has a gold earring in his left ear. He has a husky voice and is a regular at Café Wha? in Greenwich Village, New York.'

These conclusions are not trivial and contribute value to the investigation. We know that the suspect is not a woman and does not have short hair. And so on. A conclusion is valuable if it has a logical opposite alternative. At every crossroads, there must be at least two ways you can go. A conclusion is valuable if it increases the chances of choosing the correct way. Man or woman? Man. Long or short hair? Long. If there is no crossroads, the conclusions are trivial and do not add value.

Consider also these statements, taken from the annual reports of three multinational companies.

- Our new operations strategy is to implement continuous improvement.
- Respect for the individual is our core value.
- We are going to increase customer orientation.

From which crossroads did these strategic initiatives start? Which road did they not choose?

To avoid being trivial, it is important to understand clearly what lean is for and what it is not for. For which goals should we aim with the help of lean and for which should we not aim? Lean is not everything that is good, and everything good is not lean. Lean is a choice at a crossroads.

## CHAPTER 8

# The efficiency matrix

While the myriad books written on lean and TPS have a lot to offer, the plethora of definitions and usages of lean provides a rather confused picture of what lean actually is. In an attempt to clarify the situation, this chapter lays the foundation for a definition of lean by introducing a new framework that we call *the efficiency matrix*. This chapter explains the matrix, as well as what determines the various positions organisations can choose in this matrix and what characterises organisations' movements in the matrix.

## The efficiency matrix

Many definitions of lean are made at a low level of abstraction; using the fruit metaphor from chapter 7, they are at the level of green apples. The fact that organisations in many different industries are now starting to work with lean makes it necessary to have a definition of lean that is on a sufficiently high level of abstraction to ensure its applicability outside of large-volume manufacturing. In other words, we need a definition at the fruit level. The first step in building such a definition is to introduce a new framework: the efficiency matrix.

The efficiency matrix builds on the two forms of efficiency that were presented in the first part of this book and illustrates how an organisation can be classified based on (a) low respective high resource efficiency and (b) low respective high flow efficiency. The matrix below depicts four different operational states in which an organisation can find itself.

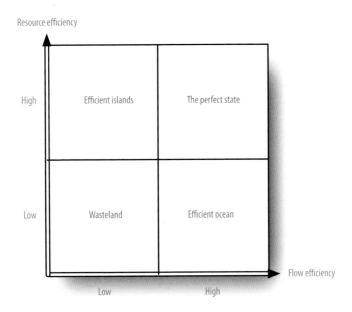

*Efficient islands*

In the top left-hand corner of the matrix is a state we call *efficient islands*. In this state, resource efficiency is high and flow efficiency is low. The organisation consists of sub-optimised parts that operate in isolation, where each part works towards maximising its resource utilisation. Through the efficient use of its own resources, each part contributes by lowering the costs for the goods or services being produced. However, efficient utilisation of resources comes at the expense of efficient flow. Flow efficiency for every individual flow unit is low. In manufacturing, this is represented by each component/product's spending most of its time as inventory. In services, this is often represented in the form of unwanted waiting time during which the customer does not receive any value.

*The efficient ocean*

In the lower right-hand corner of the matrix is a state we call the *efficient ocean*, where flow efficiency is high but resource efficiency is low. The focus is on the customer and meeting their needs as efficiently as possible. In order to maximise flow efficiency, there needs to be free capacity in the organisation's resources. Flow is efficient at the expense of an efficient use of resources. Resources are only used when there is an actual need to satisfy. Creating an efficient ocean and creating flow require a good understanding of the big picture, not just independent and efficient islands.

*Wasteland*

In the lower left-hand corner of the matrix, the organisation is unable to use its resources efficiently or create an efficient flow. Obviously, this is not a desirable state to be in because it wastes resources and creates less value for the customer. In this state, there are neither efficient islands nor an efficient ocean. It is *wasteland*, that is, poor utilisation of resources and poor flow.

*The perfect state*
In the top right-hand corner is the *perfect state*. Organisations that achieve this state have both high resource efficiency and high flow efficiency. It should be clear by now that it is difficult to reach the perfect state. The reasons why it is so difficult were explained in the discussion in chapter 3 concerning the laws that explain how processes work. Chapter 4 also discussed the difficulty by explaining the efficiency paradox. The key to the difficulty of reaching the perfect state is variation.

## Variation limits possible positions in the matrix

In order to understand what positions an organisation can achieve in the efficiency matrix, it is critical to understand variation and its impact on the organisation. Variation affects the possibility of combining high resource efficiency and high flow efficiency. We can understand the effect of variation through looking at the extreme, an organisation that utilises its resources one hundred per cent and, at the same time, meets customers' needs in an optimal way. In the figure on the next page, such an organisation would be positioned at the 'star'.

Unfortunately, the star is a theoretically perfect state, which is worth striving for but impossible to achieve. In order to reach the star, an organisation would need two things. Firstly, it would require perfect access to all information regarding the customers' present and future needs. Secondly, it would require perfectly flexible and reliable resources, where resources' capacity, functionality, and competence could be immediately

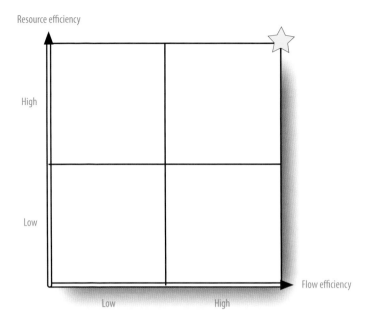

adjusted so that all types of needs could be met. Therefore, the key here is variation, both in demand (customer needs) and in supply (the organisation's resources).

*Variation in demand prevents*
*organisations from reaching the star*
The first prerequisite for being able to reach the star is perfect predictability of demand. The organisation must be able to predict perfectly:

- *What* is demanded
- *When* it is demanded
- *Which amount* is demanded

Unfortunately, a demand pattern is extremely difficult to predict. An organisation can invest time, resources, and energy in order to predict what its customers want, when they want it, and in which amount, but it will be impossible to make *perfect* predictions. It is in the nature of customer demand to be variable. Can you perfectly predict what you need, when you are going to need it, and how much? Sometimes, perhaps, but the further into the future we look, the more difficult it is.

*Variation in supply prevents organisations from reaching the star*
Even if it were possible to predict demand perfectly, reaching the star would require perfectly flexible and reliable supply. These two prerequisites concern the organisation's resources. First of all, resources must be perfectly flexible. It must be possible to adjust the capacity, functionality, and competence of resources immediately so that all types of customer needs can be met. The organisation needs perfectly flexible resources in terms of:

- *What* is supplied
- *When* it is supplied
- *Which amount* is supplied

However, it is not enough to have perfectly flexible resources. Supply must also be perfectly reliable. The organisation must always be able to predict what is going to happen when a product is produced or a service is delivered. Machines can never break down. Employees can never make mistakes, have a bad day and deliver bad service, or be sick. Suppliers must always deliver one hundred per cent quality. The IT system must never fail, and a computer must never freeze at an awkward moment. All forms of unreliability must be removed.

With perfectly flexible and reliable supply, the organisation can reach one hundred per cent resource efficiency. Regardless of *what* product or service was demanded at any time and in whatever amount, the perfect flexibility and reliability of the organisation's resources would allow it to adapt to any situation. Of course, it is impossible to have perfectly flexible and reliable supply, especially when the resources are human beings.

*Level of variation establishes the efficiency frontier*
Therefore, it is the level of variation in demand and supply that determines which operational states an organisation can achieve. Variation limits the possibilities of reaching for the star. Variation creates 'an efficiency frontier'. The notion of an efficiency frontier is illustrated in the figure below.

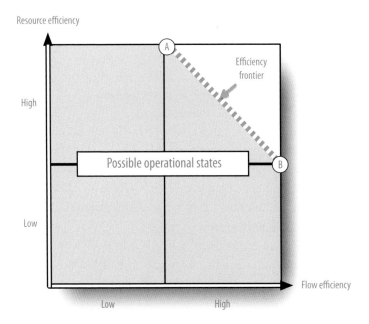

The figure on the previous page shows that the existence of variation limits the possible operational states an organisation can achieve. If demand is not perfectly predictable and/or resources are not perfectly flexible and reliable, there will be a limit to how much an organisation can improve its resource efficiency and combine it with high flow efficiency. The main point to understand here is that it is impossible to reach an operational state beyond the efficiency frontier.

Of course, it is possible for an organisation to end up in different positions within the limitation posed by the efficiency frontier. This depends on whether the organisation prioritises resource efficiency or flow efficiency. This is illustrated in the figure on the previous page through the two points, A and B.

- The organisation positioned at A has prioritised to keep its resources busy at the expense of an efficient flow.
- The organisation positioned at B has prioritised an efficient flow at the expense of having less efficient use of resources.

These are two extreme positions. An organisation can be positioned anywhere between A and B along the efficiency frontier. This will happen if the organisation prioritises a combination of resource efficiency and flow efficiency.

However, it is even more likely that the organisation will be positioned somewhere else within the shaded area. Being positioned within the efficiency frontier indicates an improvement opportunity.

Not only variation in itself, but also the level of variation, has an important effect on the efficiency matrix. The more variation there is (in demand and supply), the harder it is to combine high resource efficiency with high flow efficiency, or 'reach for the star', as the following figure shows.

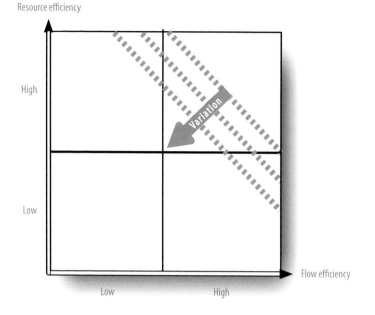

In a sense, the efficiency frontier is pushed 'inwards' as the level of variation increases. Being pushed inwards means that an organisation facing high variation will find it harder to combine high resource efficiency with high flow efficiency than an organisation facing low variation.

It is very important to understand that the efficiency frontier is pushed inwards as variation increases. Which of the two examples below would you expect to have an easier time combining high resource efficiency with high flow efficiency?

A. A manufacturing company producing large volumes of similar products.
B. The accident and emergency ward of a hospital.

The answer should be fairly evident (the correct answer is A), as these are two extreme cases. However, the key point here is that some organisations will find it inherently more difficult than others to combine high resource efficiency with high flow efficiency. Examples of organisations facing high variation are those in which the main flow unit is people. Many service organisations will fall into this category. People introduce an element of variation that is very hard, if not impossible, to avoid. We cannot standardise or control people in the same way we can material or information. However, regardless of the type of organisation, it is often possible to become better at eliminating, reducing, and managing variation.

The better an organisation is at developing capabilities to handle the two conditions, *predictability of demand* and *flexibility and reliability of supply,* the further out the organisation will move towards the star in the perfect state. The ability to handle variation is critical. Still, it is very important to note that although the level of variation decides possible positions in the efficiency matrix, an organisation can and should choose where to position itself. This is the task of strategy.

## Strategy decides position in the matrix

Many definitions of lean define it as a means rather than a goal. This disregards the important question of *why* certain activities are undertaken. To lay the foundation for a definition of lean that emphasises the goal, it is critical to understand the importance of strategic choice. Organisations have a choice regarding the position in the efficiency matrix they want to achieve. One position is not necessarily better than another.

In order to understand the importance of strategy, we must first be clear about the difference between a business strategy and an operations strategy. Simply put, a business strategy defines what type of customer need the organisation wishes to satisfy. An operations strategy defines how the organisation will meet this need.

### A business strategy defines what

The business strategy defines the value the company will offer the customer; that is, the value the customer will experience when a good or service is consumed. At the highest level of abstraction (the 'fruit' level), an organisation can either focus on differentiation or cost. In this context, differentiation includes a range of things, such as delivering a better experience, better food, faster service, or a wide range of products from which to choose. In other words, differentiation is anything that a customer considers valuable. The cost is the sacrifice, in terms of money, time, or energy, that the customer must make in order to satisfy his or her need.

A fundamental idea in the literature on business strategy is the importance of choosing between differentiation and cost. There is often a trade-off between these two strategic objectives and an organisation must prioritise one over the other or it will be stuck in the middle. Therefore, an important decision when devising a business strategy is the level of differentiation that will be offered to the customer at what cost.

Business strategy choices concern the type of need the organisation will satisfy. Business strategies are about understanding and choosing which objective to prioritise. Things that must be considered here are what the customers value, what competitors do, and what the organisation is good at doing. 'We shall offer the best customer service in our industry' is a concrete example of an objective in a business strategy.

### An operations strategy defines how

An operations strategy helps realise a business strategy and defines *how* value is to be produced. All organisations have an operations strategy, whether it is explicit or not. The operations strategy answers the question, 'How shall we produce value?' We are assuming here that we have already defined the type of need the organisation is trying to satisfy and the target market. There should be a clear link between the business strategy and the operations strategy. Given that we have defined the organisation's business strategy, we can now develop an operations strategy.

An operations strategy enables an organisation to address important questions such as, 'How will we produce a product or service given our business strategy?', 'How will the organisation deliver quality?' and, 'How will the organisation deliver low cost?' An operations strategy can be broken down into operational objectives. Resource efficiency and flow efficiency are two operational objectives defined at the highest level of abstraction, the 'fruit level'. These objectives can be broken down into several underlying objectives.

### Strategy and operational states

Strategy is an important explanation for an organisation's position in the efficiency matrix. Before illustrating the effect of strategic choice, we must first return to two of the operational states: wasteland and the perfect state.

As the name suggests, being in the wasteland is not a desirable state. After all, an organisation in such a state is wasting resources and making customers unhappy. Having said that, this state is not uncommon. Organisations that end up here usually lack routines, standards, structure, and coordination and have a very reactive behaviour, always handling unexpected problems.

At the other end of the spectrum is the perfect state, in which any organisation would like to find itself. As we have just seen, however, the level of variation and the organisation's ability to deal with it will dictate the organisation's chances of being in the perfect state.

Thus, strategy will help explain why an organisation either has efficient islands or is an efficient ocean. The examples below illustrate the importance of strategy for explaining an organisation's choice of operational state.

Ryan Air's business idea is to offer low-cost flights, and its business strategy involves prioritising cost above all other strategic goals. The business strategy is broken down into an operations strategy that prioritises resource efficiency. Resources are to be used to maximum capacity. For example, Ryan Air uses its airplanes to a greater extent than other air-lines by 'keeping them in the air'. Customers take off and land at airports in remote locations and are forced to spend a lot of time waiting, which means a lot of non-value-adding time. Instead of prioritising flow efficiency, Ryan Air clearly focuses on the operational objective of ensuring resource efficiency. The company has been very successful at this and has created an organisation that is always trying to improve its resource efficiency.

Luxury hotels follow a strategy of increasing flow efficiency and ending up in the efficient ocean. By constantly focusing on customer needs and trying to maximise customer value, the flow efficiency of these companies is high. There is always available capacity in value-adding resources in a luxury hotel.

The same is true for organisations fulfilling a need that is urgent or pressing or has to be prioritised. An example could be a fire brigade extinguishing a fire. To mobilise itself as quickly as possible, the brigade must have available capacity, including having resources on standby.

## Moving in the matrix

As we saw in chapter 7, a problem with many definitions of
lean is that they are trivial; they provide no logical opposites.
In order to lay the foundation for a non-trivial definition of
lean, it is important to understand the importance and meaning of organisations' movements in the efficiency matrix.

Many organisations say that they want to implement continuous improvement. Based on the discussion in chapter 7,
this is a trivial statement. The efficiency matrix enables us to
be much more concrete and require those organisations that
claim to have a strategy of continuous improvement to define
the direction in which they intend to improve. Movement in
the matrix can occur in two dimensions:

- Resource efficiency can be increased or decreased.
- Flow efficiency can be increased or decreased.

To illustrate the nature of movement in these two dimensions,
four fictitious stories are provided below. The movements
described in these stories can be found in the figure on the
next page.

### A. The start-up company

The start-up company sold women's clothing over the Internet.
The company had grown quickly but was finding it more and
more difficult to provide customer service. The company had
no developed routines and no standard operating procedures.
Every new customer need forced the company to 'reinvent the
wheel'. There was no organisation to speak of. Consequently,
customers started to complain. Deliveries were delayed, stock-
outs became increasingly frequent, and quality issues surfaced

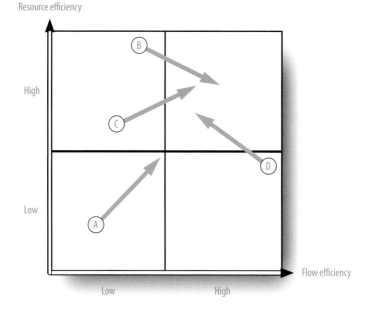

regularly. Despite lots of duplicated work, many issues were being overlooked.

A well-known venture capital company bought a stake in the company, bringing both capital and knowledge. Structure and order were brought into the company. Routines were developed, systems were created, and standard operating procedures were implemented. As a result, customer service improved dramatically and stress levels dropped among employees who no longer had to spend most of their time fighting fires.

Point A in the figure above shows the matrix movement the start-up company made. The company initially scored low on flow efficiency, as customers were not having their needs met. The company also scored low on resource efficiency, since a lot of time was spent on superfluous work. By creating routines

and standard operating procedures, the work that was performed added more value, increasing resource efficiency. But
there was also a positive effect on flow efficiency: customers
were starting to receive timely deliveries with fewer quality
problems.

### B. The bathroom refurbishing company

The bathroom refurbishing company was quite traditional in
its methods. A refurbishment would begin with builders tear-
ing out the old bathroom. When they were finished, it took a
few days before the electrician, who was busy somewhere else,
could come to prepare for new electric installations. After the
electrician had finished, there was a wait of a few more days for
the builders to complete the next step. There was another wait
when it was time for the plumber, and so on. The total time
from start to finish was rarely less than two months, during
which time customers had to find different ways of taking care
of their personal hygiene.

All of a sudden, however, the owner had a brainwave:
customers might actually be willing to pay a premium for
faster refurbishments. The changes at the company started
by increasing the coordination between the various profes-
sions, such as builders, electricians, and plumbers. Tasks were
also standardised to a larger extent to make planning easier.
Changes were initially difficult, but everyone involved soon
realised that the new organisation made their lives easier, as
they did not have to rush between jobs as often as before. As a
result of the changes, a bathroom could be refurbished in a few
weeks, and this enabled the company to charge higher prices.

Point B in the figure above illustrates the matrix movement
that the bathroom refurbishing company made. Initially,
resource efficiency was high, but flow efficiency was low.
Everyone involved in refurbishing a bathroom worked hard

and was busy, but customer service was poor. Standardising tasks, having better coordination, and freeing up capacity caused the company to lower its resource efficiency but enabled it to increase its flow efficiency. The result was happier customers and the ability to charge higher prices.

## C. The manufacturing company

The manufacturing company was a leader in its industry but was very traditional. The journey for a product from raw material to finished product would typically start with processing in one part of one factory. Due to long machine set-up times, more than two months' worth of items were produced in one batch, which resulted in high amounts of work-in-progress. Items were then shipped to the company's second factory, where they were processed in two steps before being returned to the first factory, where they were assembled.

The company responded to market changes by embarking on a large-scale manufacturing transformation. The factory layouts were changed so that groups of products were finalised at the same place. The company adopted statistical process control, and employees were trained in standard operating procedures and quality work. The hierarchical organisation, in which one person did one job, was changed into a team-based work organisation in which each person was trained to perform several jobs. Teams were also tasked with simpler forms of production planning, purchasing, and maintenance. The changes had several positive effects. Quality improved, manufacturing lead times were cut from three months to one week, and total productivity increased. Most importantly, profitability increased.

Point C in the figure above illustrates the manufacturing company's matrix movement. Initially, the company scored quite high on resource efficiency, but customers had to wait a long time to have products delivered (low flow efficiency). The change involved trying to eliminate and reduce different forms of variation in order to improve both resource efficiency and flow efficiency.

### D. The luxury hotel

This five-star hotel had always prided itself on its excellent service. The hotel offered all kinds of luxurious amenities, exquisite food, and service that was second to none. Staff were always available to fulfil their discerning guests' every wish. The intention was to create the perfect experience for the customer. The problem was that the hotel was losing money due to low average room occupancy and high staff costs.

A new owner brought widespread changes. The hotel was repositioned to target business customers and was changed to a four-star rating. Room prices were reduced, as was the number of staff, and many services were removed. The outcome was a rise in occupancy rates and higher profitability.

The hotel's matrix movement is illustrated by point D in the figure above. Initially, the hotel scored very high on flow efficiency but had relatively low resource efficiency. In order to improve profitability, it was necessary to increase resource utilisation. The decision had a negative effect on customer service (flow efficiency decreased). However, the overall effect on profitability was positive, as the decrease in customer service and revenue was more than offset by the increase in resource efficiency and consequently lower costs.

## Lean 2.0

The efficiency matrix serves as a foundation for understanding what lean is at the 'fruit level'. In order to avoid falling into the trap of making lean highly context-dependent, we want to define lean at a sufficiently high level of abstraction for it to apply to all kinds of organisations. This is important, given the interest in lean in various industries, including public sector service organisations.

The matrix highlights the importance of strategic choice. Organisations have a choice regarding where to position themselves and how to move within the matrix. An organisation can move both up and down in the matrix and to the right and to the left. Resource efficiency can be increased or decreased, and flow efficiency can be increased or decreased. There is no 'best' solution; it all depends on the organisation, its competitive environment, its customer needs and, particularly, its business strategy – what value does the organisation want to provide?

## CHAPTER 9

# This is lean!

Having an understanding of the efficiency matrix allows us to develop our definition of lean at the fruit level. We do this by using the matrix to illustrate how Toyota has implemented TPS within the car dealer operations in Japan. We then use the matrix as a conceptual lens through which we filter the example; this helps us develop a working definition of lean. In brief, lean is an operations strategy that prioritises flow efficiency over resource efficiency. In other words, lean is a strategy for moving 'to the right and up' in the efficiency matrix.

## The super-quick car inspection

Toyota's dealer network in Japan consists of approximately three hundred different car dealer companies. Together, these companies control approximately five thousand car dealerships, which usually have a *one-stop-shop approach,* offering their customer both sales and service at the same location.

Since 1996, Toyota has continuously developed a TPS-based service concept called Toyota Sales Logistics (TSL). Toyota owns only a small proportion of the car dealer companies. Therefore, the aim of the TSL concept is to assist and support all individual companies in their improvement activities through the development, spread, and implementation of TSL. The TSL concept covers all processes within a car dealership, including sales, distribution, and service. One of the service processes is the car inspection.

A car inspection is conducted three years after the purchase of a new car and every second year thereafter. The purpose of the car inspection is to check whether the car meets the current national security standards. A car inspection in Japan is very thorough and requires nearly three hours of work. Depending on the outcome of the inspection, necessary or recommended preventive adjustments are suggested, which may require parts to be adjusted or exchanged.

*The traditional, resource-efficient approach*
Traditionally, car inspections would involve a dealer employee's picking up and dropping off the car at the customer's home. However, since the technicians who carried out the car inspection were often very busy, it could sometimes take several days before the inspection started. This led to crowded parking lots. Because land is a scarce resource in Japan, there were many problems associated with over-crowded parking

lots. Cars had to be moved back and forth all the time, and vehicles were sometimes dirtied, scratched, or even damaged.

A single technician would conduct the actual car inspection; even if the actual inspection took three hours, it usually took a few days before the inspection was completed because the technician would often work with different vehicles at the same time. The actual content of the inspection was standardised by law, but the procedure had no exact sequence or routine. Every technician had his own unique approach. The lack of standards meant that the inspection process was difficult to manage and predict, which led to planning difficulties. Furthermore, the quality of the inspection varied greatly between different technicians. Still, the technicians were all working hard since they always had something to do.

The traditional car inspection also involved problems related to a lack of information, unnecessary work, errors and mistakes, waiting time for facilities or equipment, movements of technicians within the inspection area, as well as excessive and unnecessary inventory of parts. Finally, the pick-up and drop-off process required a lot of time and effort on the part of the staff at the dealership. Consequently, customers usually had to wait up to a week for their cars.

### The aim of the new approach: flow efficiency

The new process aimed to offer a car inspection whereby customers could come to the car dealer and wait in the showroom while the service was conducted. The result was a forty-five-minute-long inspection process.

A standardised process was developed in which the sequence and duration for every activity and task were fixed. All necessary tasks were identified and standardised. Standard scripts and charts were developed for every task, and everyone was thoroughly trained in order to master the new team approach.

The knowledge and capabilities of each worker were measured in a competence matrix.

Instead of having one technician conduct the entire inspection, the new approach involved a team of one inspector and two technicians. Two technicians worked together on the vehicle, with one responsible for the left-hand side and the other for the right-hand side, while the inspector controlled the progress of the whole process. A new layout was developed to eliminate the need for movements within the inspection area.

New specialised equipment – for example, a tool for changing oil – was developed to eliminate the most severe bottlenecks within the process. Various visualisation boards and sheets were also used, showing the current status of different activities and their outcomes.

The standardisation and visualisation meant that everyone would always know what to do. They also allowed everyone involved to identify easily when things were not conducted in a timely or correct manner.

The new car inspection process had several benefits. From an operational perspective, the throughput time was much faster. The number of parked cars at the shop decreased, as did the inventory level of parts. Since the length of the car inspection was fixed at forty-five minutes, capacity planning of the whole workshop became much easier. The shop was able to achieve a good balance between utilising capacity and securing free capacity in order to retain its flexibility. This provided a more stable workload and less stress for technicians, and it increased the manager's ability to control the operations.

From a customer perspective, the new approach offered a faster and much more dependable process that now took only forty-five minutes, as opposed to approximately one week. The new inspection process also offered customers the ability to observe firsthand what was happening to the car while it was being inspected. The customer could receive accurate and instant information regarding the various activities and their outcomes. This also allowed sales staff to chat with customers and further develop their relationship with them. Flexibility also increased due to increased planning ability; customers were offered flexible pick-up times and flexible scheduling for the car inspections. Customers could plan for and cancel their car inspection with shorter notice.

## Super-quick car inspection in the efficiency matrix

The following section describes the improvement of the inspection process using the efficiency matrix. The effects are illustrated in the matrix below.

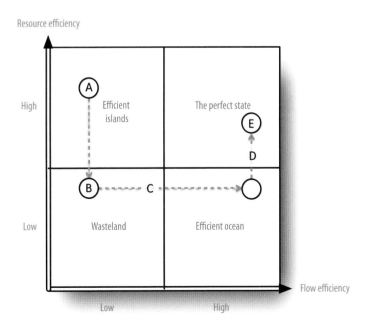

*A – Perceived starting position*

The traditional car inspection process was initially not flow-efficient. Even if the effective total value-added time were no more than three hours, the customers would commonly have to wait a week for their car. This represents a very low flow efficiency level.

The staff were busy working with various vehicles and picking up and dropping off cars at the customers' homes. The actual workshop was occupied by work-in-progress. The perception was that the technicians were resource-efficient. After all, the equipment was being utilised and everyone was working really hard, with lots of overtime logged. The starting position, as perceived by the dealer, is found at point A in the figure above: low flow efficiency and high resource efficiency.

*B – Actual starting position*

The actual starting position is found at point B. Resources were not being used as efficiently as initially believed; a lot of the work being performed was superfluous. For example, technicians performed unnecessary work and staff were busy moving the cars in the parking lot. Extra planning efforts were required because the inspection times varied so greatly.

*C – Increasing flow efficiency*

Path C indicates the initial movement the car dealer made in the matrix. The essence of the movement represents the improvement in flow efficiency. The main driving forces behind the dramatic increase in flow efficiency were teamwork, specialised equipment, standardisation, and visualisation. The speed of the value-adding activities was increased, and non-value adding activities were eliminated. Consequently, the car inspection process became faster and customers received continuous attention from the salespeople while at the workshop. Customers got what they wanted, on time, in less time, all of which indicates good flow efficiency.

### D – Increasing resource efficiency
Path D indicates how the car dealer increased its resource efficiency. The standardisation of tasks and creation of routines helped remove superfluous work, while the development of a new layout and new specialised equipment increased the resource efficiency. Resource efficiency was also improved since the creation of a common standard made capacity planning easier.

### E – Final position
The final position is found at point E. An interesting feature of the final position is that resource efficiency is less than one hundred per cent. Toyota's strategy involves having free capacity on hand in order to be able to deal with unexpected events.

### A U-shaped improvement pattern
Toyota's improvement within car dealer operations follows a U-shaped pattern. The improvement journey started at an efficient island in the northwest. It moved south and passed through the darkest valleys in wasteland, before cruising east towards the efficient ocean. It finally ended up in the northeast, where the sun is shining and the weather is beautiful. This improvement pattern, we believe, shows some key traits of lean. After all, Toyota and its TPS provided the basis for what originally lay behind the term 'lean'.

## The lean operations strategy

We see lean as an operations strategy, as it concerns how an organisation produces value. An important point here is that this strategy could be called anything: *lean* is just a word. What we call the strategy does not matter in the slightest. What matters is that the strategy involves a) aiming for the star and b) moving towards the star through moving to the right and up in the efficiency matrix, as illustrated in the figure below.

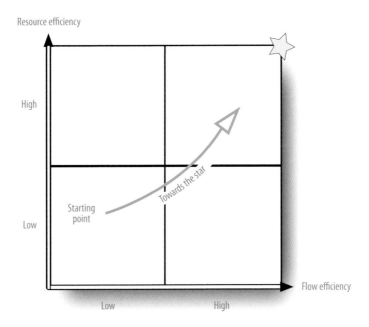

The figure illustrates that a lean operations strategy involves moving the organisation to the right in the matrix by increasing flow efficiency. In the choice between flow efficiency and resource efficiency, the first priority is clearly to focus on flow efficiency. The importance of flow efficiency is exemplified by the founding father of Toyota Production System, Taiichi Ohno, who said: 'All we are doing is looking at the time line from the moment the customer gives us an order to the point when we collect the cash'.

By focusing on flow efficiency, an organisation can also reduce a lot of superfluous work and waste. Focusing on flow efficiency helps resolve the efficiency paradox from chapter 4. Removing waste and superfluous work can improve resource efficiency, which helps an organisation move up in the matrix. A focus on flow efficiency therefore fosters an improvement of resource efficiency.

It is crucial to note that a lean operations strategy involves focusing on flow efficiency before resource efficiency, not the other way round. Focusing on resource efficiency first tends to create efficient but sub-optimised islands. Superfluous work and waste often occur between the islands. A focus on flow efficiency means an integration of the separate islands to one integrated system. This integrated system serves as the basis for increasing resource efficiency. Resource efficiency is improved at a system level, not at the level of individual islands.

By now, it is hopefully clear that what prevents organisations from reaching the perfect state is variation. Therefore, it is vital in a lean operations strategy to eliminate, reduce, and manage variation. The knowledge that it is not possible to reach the theoretical state of perfection (the star) means that a lean operations strategy implies always striving to get closer to that state through continuous improvement.

## Away from the Wild West

Chapter 7 defined three problems with the numerous different definitions of lean. First, lean is defined at different levels of abstraction. Second, lean is seen as a means instead of an end. Third, lean is everything that is good, and everything good is lean. We have dealt with those problems by defining lean as an operations strategy:

a. The definition is at the *fruit level,* which is a high level of abstraction. Increasing the level of abstraction helps make lean applicable in different environments. Everything can be linked to a goal.

b. The definition focuses on the *goal of flow efficiency,* not the means. The point is not to copy what Toyota does or copy TPS. Instead, it is important to understand *why* Toyota and other organisations that focus on flow efficiency do what they do. Only then can your organisation do the same.

c. The definition is *non-trivial* and makes it possible to define what *lean is* and *what lean is not.* The definition clearly shows that flow efficiency is prioritised above the efficient use of resources.

Our goal in attempting to deal with these three problems is to avoid a context-specific definition of lean. 'Lean' is just a term that was created by Western researchers who observed Toyota's efficiency. It is important to emphasise that the means Toyota has used to increase flow efficiency may not be applicable in every environment. How a lean operations strategy will be realised will depend on the context. A solution that suits one organisation or environment will not necessarily be suitable in another organisation or environment.

By defining lean as an operations strategy, we aim to show that lean is a strategic choice for all organisations. Organisations in all environments can benefit from better flow efficiency and, in the longer term, also increase their resource efficiency. To work out whether this is something your organisation should strive for, it is important to look first at your business strategy and ask, 'What value do we want to create, and how should we compete?'

## CHAPTER 10

# Realising a lean operations strategy

L ean is an operations strategy, a strategy to achieve an objective. In particular, the objective is to prioritise high flow efficiency over resource efficiency. Having said that, by eliminating, reducing, and managing variation, the aim is continually to increase both flow efficiency and resource efficiency. But how does an organisation become lean? This is a legitimate question, but is it the *right* question?

## The naïve foreigner

It is a warm morning in Nagoya. Three researchers from the University of Tokyo walk across the polished marble floor of a fifty-storey building, enter the lift, and press the button for the twenty-second floor: 'Toyota Motor Corporation – Reception'.

The researchers register at reception, are each given a name badge, and are then politely pointed in the direction of another lift, which will take them to the forty-second floor. They are soon to meet Nishida-san, senior manager for the internal special unit that Toyota started in 1995 to develop concepts for increasing efficiency in sales, distribution, and service of Toyota cars.

Nishida-san is one of the younger senior managers at Toyota. Despite having worked in various roles within the company for over thirty-seven years, he still has a lot to learn about the Toyota Production System. Toyota's internal training programme takes twenty-five years to complete; as Nishida-san himself admitted, he knows little more than the basics.

Nishida-san wears a classically cut green-grey Armani suit. His manner makes it clear that he is the one who calls the shots, definitely ahead of the three other managers who follow him into the meeting room. Nobody interrupts Nishida-san, nobody disagrees with him, and nobody walks in front of him.

The Toyota men greet their visitors in a calm and orderly manner and exchange business cards with the pride and reverence that you would associate with a wedding gift to the emperor. After a short presentation by each participant, Nishida-san asks a question that is specifically aimed at the one non-Japanese researcher.

'You are the first foreign researcher to visit us. Why are you here?'

The foreigner answers nervously in broken Japanese:

'I am from Sweden, and I carry out research in lean service. I am researching how service organisations apply lean in their businesses. You have developed many tools and methods that have made your production process one of the most efficient in the world. Can you tell me how you implement them in your service business? For example, how have you adapted the tools and methods for your sales and service processes?'

Nishida-san looks blankly down at the table, then sighs and looks up again. His expression is reminiscent of a Samurai warrior about to attack, but he sounds calm when he replies:

'Yet another foreigner who does not understand anything.'

After a moment's silence, he continues:

'You have just asked a question that shows you do not understand what TPS is about. Foreigners created the concept of lean, which was a summary of what they saw in our factories, of our tools and methods. They completely missed what they did *not* see. Our philosophy. They missed the soft and invisible that explains why we use the tools and methods that we do.'

'If you are going to be here for two years, I recommend that you try to focus on and try to understand our core philosophy. Our values and our principles guide us in everything we do. If you understand them, then you will also understand how we improve the efficiency in our service processes.'

Nishida-san stood up, walked over to the whiteboard, and drew a circle at the top of what would become a pyramid-like figure. Beside the circle he wrote the word 'values'.

'Let me use a metaphor to help you understand. When we established Toyota Motor Corporation, we saw our company as a newly planted tree. At that time we had no knowledge of

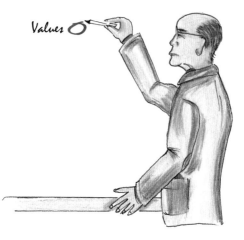

how to take care of and look after a tree. Our lack of knowledge led us to be very careful. We never made a hasty decision. We asked ourselves questions such as:

- What do we consider a beautiful tree?
- What do we not consider a beautiful tree?'

'When we had a consensus around those questions, we summarised our thoughts into our values. Those values defined how we should always be towards our tree.'

'The most important value was always to focus on the customer. To satisfy our customers' needs. Satisfying our customers' needs was the same thing as a beautiful tree. Customer needs were placed above all else. By satisfying our customers, we could get our tree to grow. The customer was most important and should be prioritised above all else.'

'Our values became a source from which all of our co-workers could seek guidance. In those values, you can find all the answers to how we should act in every situation. Those values show us how we should always be. They became the core of our culture.'

Nishida-san continued to develop the figure on the white-board. He drew two more circles beneath the first one, and from the first circle he drew two arrows pointing down to the other two circles. Beside these new circles he wrote the word 'principles' and then continued talking:

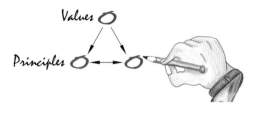

'As our tree continued to grow, we continued to look after it according to our values. To ensure that we really did look after it, we asked ourselves questions such as:

- What decisions have we made today that made the tree more beautiful?
- What decisions have we made today that did not make the tree more beautiful?
- What can we learn from this to ensure that the tree will be even more beautiful tomorrow?'

'By asking ourselves these questions every day, principles gradually started to develop regarding how we made decisions. We started to see a pattern around how we looked after our tree so that its beauty was always growing. The principles guided us in terms of how and what we should prioritise in our business. The principles developed due to our attention's always being on our values. You could say that our principles realised our values as they guided us in looking after our tree, but also in how *not* to look after our tree.'

Under the lower left circle, Nishida-san wrote: 'Just-in-time'.

'After a long development process, we understood that our thoughts could be summarised into two principles, which were two sides of the same coin.'

'The first principle is just-in-time and is about creating flow. Imagine a football match. Flow is when the team passes the ball from one end of the pitch to the other and finally kicks the ball into the opponents' goal. The ball is moving all the time. All the players help to find the perfect path for the ball. The ball flows across the pitch and into the goal. In principle, scoring a goal in football is the same as delivering exactly what the customer wants, when the customer wants it, and in the quantity that the customer wants. Customer service is about scoring a goal.'

Nishida-san went quiet again and turned back to the whiteboard. Under the lower right circle he wrote another word: 'Jidoka'.

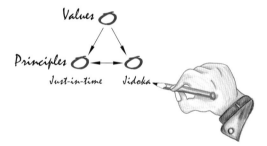

'Jidoka is the other side of the same coin. It complements just-in-time. Jidoka is a somewhat abstract principle, but let me ask a question that will hopefully help you to grasp it. What underlying conditions must exist in order for a football team to score a lot of goals?'

The researchers looked at each other and wondered if Nishida-san was winding them up. Nonetheless, they started to offer some answers:

'Good playing tactics! Great kicks!'

'Strength and speed!'

'Teamwork and passing ability!'

Nishida-san gave a satisfied smile and said:

'You answered exactly how I expected you to answer, and you
are all wrong. You focus too much on the conditions that need
to exist to create a good flow. Jidoka is much simpler than that.
In football, the answer is so obvious that we do not think about
it as a condition.'

'In addition to all the players being able to understand the rules
and their own team's strategy, all the players, from all positions
on the pitch, must always be able to:

- See the pitch
- See the ball
- See the goal
- See all players on the pitch
- See the score
- See how much playing time is left
- Hear the whistle
- Hear their team members and the crowd'

'Every player can see and hear and is aware of everything that
is happening all the time. Based on this clear picture they can
make decisions about how, together, they can score a goal. If
any player makes a mistake, or if one of the teams scores a goal,
the referee blows his whistle. All players hear this whistle, and
the game stops. These conditions are the same in most team

sports. Everyone can see everything all the time and the referee can stop the game within a second.'

It went quiet in the room and it was apparent that everyone was thinking about what Nishida-san had just said.

> 'In an organisation, it is much more difficult to create these fundamental underlying conditions. We all sit in different places, and we do different things at different times, independently of each other. Today's organisations are built like a football pitch covered in hundreds of small tents, where matches are played with many different balls at the same time. The players are rewarded for kicking the ball as many times as they can and think they score a goal when they succeed in kicking the ball out of their own tent. They play at different times and barely know the names of the other players. No one sees the big picture. No one hears the whistle.'

Nishida-san drew another arrow on the figure, between *just-in-time* and *jidoka*. He went on to say:

> 'Just-in-time is about creating flow, while jidoka is about creating a visible and clear picture so that anything that happens to, hinders or disturbs the flow can be identified immediately. The principles are two sides of the same coin and together they drive our organisation to "score goals" continually through strong customer focus.'

Nishida-san again turned to the whiteboard and drew another level of circles. He connected the six new circles to the two above with some more arrows. Everything hung together. Beside the new circles he wrote 'methods'.

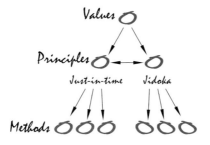

'As we developed our business, by allowing the principles to direct all that we did we started to see patterns.'

'This time, it was not about patterns of how we were or how we made decisions, but patterns of what we did and how we carried out different tasks. Regardless of what we did, we always concentrated on realising just-in-time and jidoka. As time went on, we started to identify how we should carry out different tasks. Some methods emerged as being better than others. Therefore, we tried to identify, standardise, and spread the best way of doing different tasks. That resulted in many standardised methods; the collation of our jointly devised best thoughts about how different tasks should be performed. These methods standardised how we could realise our principles in different situations in the best way possible.'

'Methods were our best way of looking after our tree every day so that it could be as beautiful as possible. Let me give you an example. To realise just-in-time, we developed many different methods that helped us continually ensure that we delivered what the customers want, when they want it, and in just the amount that they wanted.'

'Standardisation itself is an example of one of our most important methods. It is actually a method of developing other methods. In order to create and – most importantly – maintain an efficient flow, the flow must be standardised at some point so that everyone can have the same understanding of how a task should be carried out. But how do you standardise something? How do you establish one best way of working? The challenge here is the same as it is in football. How is it possible for a football manager to establish a standardised attack method? Standardisation is a standard for establishing standards. A meta-standard!'

Nishida-san grinned at the foreigner.

'We have been able to develop several methods that help realise just-in–time and jidoka. Visual planning is an example of a method needed to realise jidoka. As I said, the intention of jidoka is to create a transparent organisation so that everyone can see everything all the time. That is made possible through visualising and continually updating all of the relevant information concerning the business on our walls. Everyone can see what is happening in our company in just one look. Visual planning is a method that helped realise jidoka.'

The researchers didn't really appear to get the point Nishida-san was making. The Toyota manager continued in a slightly louder voice.

'It is important that you really understand the reasons *why* we visualise. Think about jidoka! We want to see the whole picture all the time. If all employees visualise the progress they are making, two particular things are made possible. First, if the progress is going according to plan, we know that we are on track. The visualised information allows us to see that the situation is normal. We are doing what we are supposed to be doing. Secondly, if the progress is not going according to plan, the visualised information enables us to react instantly. We can see that the situation is abnormal. We see deviations from the normal state.'

'Do you understand? It is the visualisation that allows us to see the whole football pitch all the time. It is impossible to control a whole organisation. But it is possible to standardise and visualise everything we do. Through visualisation, we can control the whole organisation by just controlling the deviations from the standards. It is the deviations that trigger improvement of the normal state.'

The room was quiet.

Nishida-san continued to add to the pyramid on the whiteboard. He drew a final layer of circles, this time twelve of them, and connected them to the others in the same way as he had done earlier. Again, he wrote something beside the circles, but quickly rubbed it out and turned to the researchers.

'What is this here?'

He turned back to the whiteboard and hit it with his hand.

'WHAT is this here?'

Nishida-san hit the whiteboard several times more and then stared at the researchers. No one had any idea what answer he was looking for. Finally the hitting stopped and Nishida-san spoke to the researchers slowly and clearly:

'It is a *whiteboard,* and I am *hitting* it. It constitutes a method I developed a minute ago, which is called *the method that will stop the researchers from falling asleep.'*

Nishida-san laughed in a way that indicated he was satisfied. He went back to his pyramid. Next to the lowest level of rings he wrote the words *tools* and *activities*.

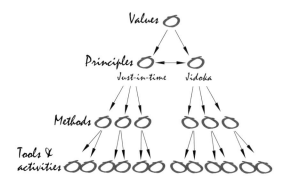

'The whiteboard is a tool. The hitting is an activity. Tools and activities are how methods are realised. A method is built up of activities (what we do) and tools (what we have).'

'To carry out the method of standardisation, we have developed an A3 template that is divided into different boxes. It is used to document a standard. The template is a tool that we need in order to standardise. We have also defined the sequence of activities that an employee goes through to fill in the template. Tools and activities are the components of the methods.'

Nishida-san took a step back from the whiteboard and looked proudly at his creation. He turned to the researchers and explained.

'Our values define how we should be, regardless of the situation or context. Values are the basis for our very existence and the state towards which we continually strive.'

'Our principles define how we should make decisions and what we should prioritise. Just-in-time and jidoka define the direction in which our operations should develop. Towards the customer! Towards that beautiful tree!'

'The methods define how we should perform different tasks. Methods are the motors that propel us in the right direction.'

'Tools are what we need to *have* and activities are what we need to *do* to realise a specific method.'

'Everything is connected in a system that, continuously and in small steps, develops our business into a very beautiful tree.'

Nishida-san went back to his seat and sat down. He looked back towards the whiteboard and then turned to the foreigner:

'So there. Now you have just had a crash course in the Toyota Production System. Pay special attention to the word "system". It is a system in which everything is connected. I hope that you managed to grasp what I have said.'

The Swedish researcher nodded nervously and expressed his gratitude by bowing in his seat. Nishida-san smiled mischievously and posed a final question:

'I will give you one last chance. Rephrase your question so that I have the chance to think, 'Wow! Finally a foreigner who really understands what TPS is!"

Nishida-san leaned back in his chair with a look of hopeful anticipation, and he turned his gaze once more on the foreigner.

## Means for realising a lean operations strategy

The story that Nishida-san told the naïve foreigner illustrates that the question, 'How does an organisation adapt the lean tools and methods for sales and service processes?' is somewhat misleading because it assumes that lean is a collection of methods and tools. Lean is not methods and tools and nor is it principles, contrary to popular belief. As we have mentioned earlier, we see lean as an operations strategy, as a strategy with which to achieve a goal. Therefore, the question should really be, 'How do we realise a lean operations strategy?' The answer to *that* question is that there are various means with which to realise a lean operations strategy.

We can refine the question further to, 'What means can we use to realise a lean operations strategy?' and 'Which means will increase flow efficiency without compromising and will preferably increase resource efficiency?' As the Nishida-san story shows, there are many different means, which can be divided into the four different groups that Nishida-san wrote on the whiteboard:

- Values define how an organisation should *behave*.
- Principles define how an organisation should *think*.
- Methods define what an organisation should *do*.
- Tools define what an organisation should *have*.

Nishida-san's pyramid shows how the different means are defined on different levels of abstraction. Values are at the highest level of abstraction and tools at the lowest. A lean operations strategy can be realised in different ways, from a more abstract change, where values are integrated and principles applied, to a more concrete change, where methods and tools are implemented. Some organisations that work with lean choose to focus on one or a few of the above levels, while others choose to focus on all of them.

The various means for realising a lean operations strategy tie in well with the existing literature. Most of the books on TPS or lean are full of excellent suggestions of means to realise a lean operations strategy. Obviously we can learn a lot from the existing literature. But it is important to emphasise that all those values, principles, methods, and tools that you find in the books are not in themselves 'lean'. They are means for realising a lean

operations strategy. To see them as means does not make them
any less valuable; in fact, just the opposite is true.

By seeing all these values, principles, methods, and tools as
means, we can begin to see how everything fits together. This
helps us sort through the disparate and sometimes opposing
advice we get from studying other peoples' lessons. It helps us
to see how everything fits together.

Anything that helps us eliminate, reduce, and manage the
variation in an organisation is a good means with which to realise a lean operations strategy. Integrating values reduces variation in how we are. Applying principles reduces the variation
related to how we prioritise and make decisions. Standardising
methods decreases the variation regarding what we do.
Implementing tools reduces the variation in what we have.

It is important to understand that all organisations have
values, principles, methods, and tools, whether they want to
or not. The questions are what they consist of, how explicit
they are, and how widely accepted they are in the organisation.

## How different means realise a lean strategy

In order for means to realise a lean operations strategy, the
intention must be to eliminate, reduce, and manage variation,
primarily in order to increase flow efficiency; that is a condition. Here are a few examples of what we mean, using Toyota
as an example.

### Values as means
Values define how an organisation should behave. Which values does an organisation need to integrate in order to improve
flow efficiency? As we mentioned in chapter 6, Toyota codified
five core values in The Toyota Way. Two of these, respect and

teamwork, are clear conditions for the creation of an efficient flow.

- Respect is about doing everything to be able to understand each other. Take responsibility and do your best to create mutual trust.
- Teamwork is about stimulating personal and professional development, sharing opportunities for development, and maximising individual and group achievement.

By training employees to respect each other and work as a team, these values become integrated in an organisation. This creates the conditions for efficient flow throughout the entire organisation. Respect and teamwork are prerequisites for achieving high flow efficiency since everyone is dependent on each other and has to work together.

*Principles as means*
Principles define how people in an organisation should think in order to increase flow efficiency. Which principles should you apply in order to eliminate, reduce, and manage the variation that exists in your organisation?

The Nishida-san story discusses the two principles that Toyota consider to be the core of TPS: just-in-time and jidoka. Just-in-time means creating an efficient flow through the whole organisation. Jidoka means creating an *aware* organisation, which prevents, identifies, and eliminates everything that inhibits, disrupts, or slows down the flow.

These are the two principles that guide Toyota. They are at the core of the company's way of creating flow. Therefore, an organisation can choose to apply just these two principles when developing its operations, but it could equally choose to apply other flow-improving principles. In order to realise a lean operations strategy, it is not important *how* the flow is improved, simply that it is improved.

Many observers have considered the global truck company Scania to be a role model for lean. Inspired by Toyota, Scania started to develop its own version of lean, the Scania Production System (SPS), in the early 1980s. Instead of just-in-time and jidoka, the core of SPS consists of four principles, the objectives of which are almost identical to just-in-time and jidoka, except that they are conceptualised differently. Scania and Toyota both have operations strategies that focus on flow efficiency, except that Scania realises its strategy through SPS, while Toyota uses TPS. They use different means but have the same goal.

*Methods as means*

Methods define what an organisation should do in order to improve flow efficiency. Among the many different methods to choose from is value stream mapping. Toyota has developed this method to analyse the existing flow in a process, with a view to identifying value-adding activities and non-value-adding activities (waste). Other organisations can copy and standardise value stream mapping as a method of analysing flow in their existing processes.

Another common method that is often seen as part of lean is 5s (sorting, structuring, shining, standardising, and sustaining). Simply put, 5s is about having the right thing in the right place. Many organisations start to use 5s as a method to create a well-organised and functioning workplace. Well-organised workplaces reduce the variation that can easily arise when you have to spend time looking for what you need.

*Tools as means*

Finally, tools define what an organisation has. So what tools need to be implemented in order to realise a lean operations strategy? Visual planning boards are one of the most common tools associated with Toyota. The intention is to make the progress of the process visible through visualising process-oriented and result-oriented metrics. Is the flow normal or does it deviate from the normal? By implementing and using a visual planning board, an organisation can see and control the status of the flow through the process. As soon as a deviation is identified, it can be dealt with.

## Means are not universal

When means for realising a lean operations strategy are seen as being on different levels of abstraction, it is possible to understand better that means are context dependent:

- The higher the level of abstraction, the less context-dependent the means.
- The lower the level of abstraction, the more context-dependent the means.

In this case, context is determined by the type of organisation in which the means have been developed. Tools as means are at the lowest level of abstraction, which means that they are the most dependent on context. Tools for realising a lean operations strategy, developed in a particular context, are not necessarily applicable in another context. This does not mean that lean is not appropriate, just that the tool is not.

It is important to bear in mind that Toyota's means were developed within a manufacturing industry, which is characterised by high volumes and relatively little variation in the product's basic design. Most organisations could draw inspiration from Toyota's means and learn about what Toyota has done. However, not all organisations, particularly those operating in different environments from Toyota's, can or should copy all the methods and tools that Toyota developed.

This is in line with Toyota's own view that methods and tools are 'countermeasures'; they are solutions to problems that the company has faced during its work to improve flow efficiency. Today, these are the best solutions to Toyota's problems, but tomorrow's solutions may look different. This view explains why Toyota is happy to let other organisations learn more about the methods and tools it works with and uses.

For many organisations, realising a lean operations strategy is about developing solutions, methods, and tools to help them eliminate, reduce, and manage the variation that exists in the context in which they work. This development work should be inspired by others, but should not indiscriminately copy what others have done.

By really understanding what lean is, organisations can find their own solutions to the problems they encounter when trying to improve flow efficiency and strive towards the perfect state.

## CHAPTER 11

# Are you lean?
# Learn to fish!

Thereare many different means with which to real-ise a lean operations strategy. Organisations can integrate values to help improve flow efficiency. Principles can be applied to help employees constantly make decisions that improve flow efficiency. Methods can be standardised and tools implemented, all with a view to eliminating, reducing, and managing variation in the organisation. This improves flow efficiency and, at the same time, allows a more efficient use of resources. But with all this work, how can we tell that an organisation has become lean?

## We are lean, aren't we?

The European engineering company was very proud of its
work on lean, and justifiably so. Within its industry, it was
considered the company that had come the furthest in its work
on lean. Many study visits took place at the company, and
many other organisations were eager to learn from this great
company and its experiences with lean.

The employees were very proud of their company but were
still eager to know if there were something more they could
develop. What should they do in order to take the company
to the next level? Was there a next level or was the company
perfectly lean?

In order to confirm just how good it was, the company invited
Ooba-san, a legendary Toyota manager. Ooba-san had served
as the right-hand man to the even more legendary Ohno-san,
considered to be the father of the Toyota Production System.

Ooba-san was flown in to assess the engineering company's
work on lean. He arrived and was given a guided tour of the
factory. The company's representatives proudly showed off
their work. They showed their clean work places, where everything was in its right place. They showed their visual planning
boards, where all aspects of how the business was working were
shown in real time. They talked proudly of their low levels of
inventory in the factory. They showed the different tools they
used to raise the level of quality.

'We are lean, aren't we?' asked one of the company's representatives rhetorically, but the Japanese visitor simply said,
'Interesting'.

Ooba-san even had the chance to speak with operators
working in the factory. Everyone he spoke to had the same
understanding of the company's visions and goals. Everyone
could provide answers about how their work fitted in with

the work of the business as a whole and how their work contributed to the final product delivered to the customer. The operators explained with genuine enthusiasm the improvement work with which they were involved.

'This just has to be lean, doesn't it?' asked the company's managers. Again, Ooba-san simply responded by saying, 'Interesting'.

After the guided tour, everyone who had accompanied Ooba-san congregated in the conference room where the discussions continued. The company's representatives were eager to obtain some confirmation from Ooba-san about how lean their company was. However, no answer was forthcoming, and the frustration in the room began to increase. Finally, the chairman said:

> 'Ooba-san, we have now shown you the whole factory and told you about our work on lean, which we are very proud of. We are wondering now if you consider this to be world-class lean?'

Ooba-san's answer was short and to the point.

> 'It is impossible for me to say. I wasn't here yesterday.'

## When is a lean operations strategy realised?

The story about Ooba-san illustrates a central aspect of lean: namely, that lean is not a static state to reach. It is not something you complete. It is a dynamic state characterised by constant improvement.

If we see lean as an operations strategy, the question, 'When are we lean?' is actually the wrong one. Instead, the question should be, 'When is a lean operations strategy realised?' The goal of a lean operations strategy is to improve the flow efficiency, without sacrificing resource efficiency, and ideally improving it. The strategy would be realised when the goal is achieved. There are two extreme ways of defining a goal: static or dynamic.

### An operations strategy with a static goal

From a static perspective, the development of a lean operations strategy involves setting a definite goal for flow efficiency. Improvement is then seen as a project, a transformation of one or more processes with the intention of implementing a substantial improvement of flow efficiency. When a change project has a definite goal, flow efficiency is measured before and after the change. The degree to which the flow efficiency has improved can then be used to determine the success of a specific project. The measurement can also be used for internal and external comparison, through questions such as, 'Where and when is the flow most efficient?' The figure below illustrates an operations strategy with a static goal.

The figure illustrates a project that, over a specific time period, improved the absolute level of flow efficiency. The figure shows the change from one static state to another.

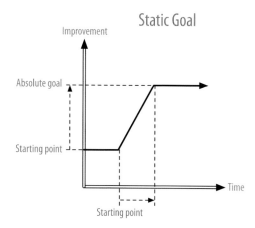

As the story about Ooba-san illustrates, the static view is not the right one. The fact that many organisations see lean as something that can be implemented, at which point they can say, 'We've done it now', is a legacy of the often unarticulated tool-based and methods-focused definition of lean. Of course, a lean journey can comprise of and be broken down into smaller projects that can have clear milestones. However, it is crucial to understand that the realisation of a lean operations strategy is a journey that never ends. Let us expand on this.

*An operations strategy with a dynamic goal*
From a dynamic perspective, the focus is not on the absolute improvement in the level of flow efficiency; instead, the point is that flow efficiency always continues to improve over time. Taking the dynamic view means that an organisation sees the realisation of a lean operations strategy as a constantly changing state, not as something static. In this case, a lean operations strategy is realised when an organisation continuously improves its flow efficiency. The figure below illustrates the dynamic view.

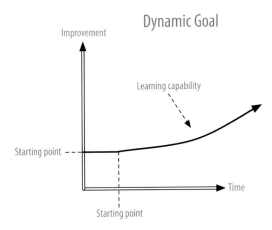

The figure shows that the goal is not on the vertical axis. It is not the absolute level that is most important. The upswing of the curve illustrates the dynamic state, which is all about continuous improvement.

## The continuously improving organisation

The story about Ooba-san illustrates Toyota's view on realising a lean operations strategy, which is about creating an organisation that continuously improves flow. The only way of determining whether an organisation is lean is by comparing how an organisation operates at two separate points in time. The organisation is in a dynamic state if it can show constant improvement.

Realising a lean operations strategy is not just about improving the actual flow; it is also about continuously improving in different ways. The continuously flow-improving organisation will always be developing new knowledge, new understanding, and new experiences and learning new things about its customers' needs and how to meet those needs as efficiently as possible.

'What have we done during this project?' is the question that would be asked from a static perspective. An organisation taking a dynamic perspective would ask, 'How do we ensure that we learn something new every day?'

This view of realising a lean operations strategy is about as far as you can get from the view that lean consists of a series of tools to be implemented.

## Catching the big fish or learning to fish?

This discussion around a static or dynamic goal raises a key question: 'How should we think about improvement?'

The classic view of improvement is in line with the static view. An organisation feels that it has a problem; we can liken this problem to 'a big fish'. The organisation invests lots of resources into catching this big fish. Therefore, the goal of the improvement project is to 'catch the fish'. Regardless of whether it is external consultants, internal consultants, or employees that carry out the improvement work, the project is finished when 'the fish is caught'. There is a beginning and an end.

Toyota's view of improvement is in line with the dynamic view. Toyota's basic view is that there are always going to be problems. The key is to ensure that all employees know how to fish and Toyota's improvement projects are geared towards 'teaching employees to fish'. Everyone can always improve their fishing ability, as there will always be new fish. Large and small. Fast and slow. Easily caught and not so easily caught. What is central is the organisation's ability to fish. So if there is to be a beginning and an end in an improvement project, the focus would be on the ability to fish, not on the fish itself.

Before embarking on a change process, it is important for an organisation to ask itself what view it has of improvement. 'How should we think about improvement? Shall we catch the big fish or shall we learn to fish?' Anyone can catch the big fish. Learning how to become a 'self-fishing' organisation is something completely different.

# Develop a lean outfit!

Imagine you have a huge pile of clothes on the floor. There are trousers and skirts, shirts and blouses, socks and underwear. Different types of clothes for different occasions and different purposes. Clothes for everyday use, for parties, for jogging, and for work.

The pile of clothes is a mess and gets bigger as you buy more clothes. Eventually, the pile grows so high that it becomes difficult to find the right garment for the right occasion. It takes a long time to find the right piece of clothing, and you really have to search for it. You have simply lost the overview of your clothes. It is nearly impossible to find the perfect outfit for the party on Friday. You need a system for sorting.

Clothes are a metaphor for all the knowledge published on lean and Toyota. We have never intended to criticise this knowledge; in fact, this knowledge is incredibly important. However, the knowledge has grown increasingly quickly in recent years. The stock of knowledge has become enormous and overgrown. Just as it is hard to find the right garment in the huge pile of clothes, it is difficult to find the right knowledge for your organisation.

*This Is Lean* is an attempt to create a sorting system. We hope that the book serves as a wardrobe to help you sort out your pile of clothes. We want it to help you quickly find the blouse for the meeting, your sandals for the beach, and your hat for the first cold winter day. The right garment for the right occasion.

Continuing with the clothes metaphor, by remaining at a high level of abstraction this book has attempted to define what a certain type of clothing is and what it isn't. These are trousers, and those are not trousers. This is a lean operations strategy, and that is not a lean operations strategy. We have argued that a lean operations strategy focuses on flow efficiency. This means that an operations strategy that focuses on resource efficiency is not lean.

Our intention has not been to recommend a specific operations strategy. It is important to be aware that resource efficiency and flow efficiency both have their own advantages and disadvantages. We do not want to suggest a particular garment, but we do want to suggest you make an informed choice. We are unable to answer the question of which operations strategy is the best one for your organisation. The choice of operations strategy must always be linked to the choice of business strategy. The more an organisation understands what these different choices mean, the higher the likelihood that the choice will be the right one.

Therefore, we have tried to create an understanding of how to sort the clothes so that they are easier to find. Some clothes are for everyone, while others are only for some people. We have described different means for realising a lean operations strategy. Values and principles, methods and tools, abstract and concrete, general and specific: no two operations strategies can be realised in exactly the same way.

The aim of this book is to help organisations sort and create better order out of everything that has been written on lean and TPS. Just as a wardrobe makes it easier to find the right item of clothing for the right occasion, we hope this book has made it easier to find what is right and what isn't right for an individual organisation. Our role as researchers is to create structure (which we call 'theories') to make sense of the world around us.

This book has sought to create clarity and make it easier to realise a lean operations strategy. Clarity is a good start, but it is still a huge challenge to realise a lean operations strategy. Changing a resource-efficient organisation into a flow-efficient organisation requires change on many different levels, such as the organisational structure, control systems, incentive systems, career structures, and recruitment processes. There is no quick and simple solution. Getting an entire organisation to change its focus from resource efficiency to flow efficiency and to get all employees to think constantly about how the flow can be improved places huge demands on leadership.

Toyota employees willingly share their tools and methods and are happy to talk about their principles and values. Nonetheless, it is difficult to understand how and why Toyota has repeatedly succeeded in creating self-fishing organisations all around the world, where the flow improves over time, all the time. This knowledge is difficult to decode and has taken nearly a hundred years to develop. Toyota's wardrobe is never full, complete, or ready. But Toyota's employees are the best in the world at asking the following question:

'Is there any little adjustment that can make us a little bit more beautiful than we were yesterday?'

# Notes

To allow the book to flow, we have opted to put the references at the end. We have also provided suggestions for further reading for readers who are particularly interested in certain topics. There is a lot of very good literature on lean, and this book has only been able to cover the basics.

## Prologue

Although the stories about Alison and Sarah are fictitious, all of the statistical data in them, such as the forty-two days and the two hours, are based on real-life cases. The stories are based on secondary data and have been thoroughly checked by five people within the Swedish healthcare industry.

Alison's diagnostic process represents a traditional process. It is important to point out that there are differences in the exact order between steps and exactly how the information flows in the process. There are differences within countries, but also between countries. To the best of our knowledge, however, the description reasonably matches a generic diagnostic process for breast cancer in many countries. The intention is not to be exact, but to point to a particular way of organising a diagnostic process that is commonly used in many healthcare systems around the world for various medical conditions.

There are several examples of similarities between what we have described in the story of Sarah and various clinics in different countries. However, Sarah's diagnostic process is taken directly from the One-Stop Breast Clinic trial that was run at Skåne University Hospital in Southern Sweden. The trial started in April 2004 but was disbanded in 2009. For more details on this trial, we can recommend the following publications (both of which are only available in Swedish, unfortunately):

Niklas Källberg, Helena Bengtsson and Jon Rognes (2011), 'Tid eller pengar: Vad fokuseras det på vid styrning av vård' (Time or Money: What is the Focus when Controlling Healthcare?), *LHC Report 1-2011*. Accessible online at www.leadinghealthcare.se.

Ingrid Ainalem, Birgitta Behrens, Lena Björkgren, Susanne Holm and Gun Tranström (2009), *Från funktion till process till patientprocess – Bröstmottagningen, ett exempel* (From Function to Process to Patient Process – the One-Stop Breast Clinic Example), Lunds Tekniska Högskola, Lund.

## Chapter 1

There is an almost unlimited source of references pointing to the importance of efficient utilisation of resources for economic development. As early as 1776, Adam Smith pointed out how division of labour could drastically increase the number of pins produced per person. Smith showed that dividing the tasks that go into making pins into eighteen different steps and having workers specialise on single subtasks could result in a drastic increase in productivity.

Adam Smith (1776/1937), *An Inquiry into the Nature and Causes of the Wealth of Nations*, Modern Library, New York.

The importance of efficiently utilising resources received a lot of attention in the early 1900s. One of the main contributors to this was Frederick Winslow Taylor, the founding father of the extremely influential scientific management movement, which affects organisations to this day. While Taylor made many important contributions, in one particular study he experimented with variously sized shovels to determine the optimum shovel load for workers. A common denominator in all his work was the focus on utilising resources in the form of individual workers and machines.

> Frederick Winslow Taylor (1919), *The Principles of Scientific Management*, Harper Brothers, New York.

## Chapter 2

For an excellent but slightly technical description of processes in organisations and their characteristics, please see:

> Ravi Anupindi, Sunil Chopra, Sudhakar D. Deshmukh, Jan A. Van Mieghem and Eitan Zemel (2012), *Managing Business Process Flows* (3rd edition), Prentice Hall, Upper Saddle River, New Jersey.

An example of an author who argues there are a finite and small number of processes in an organisation is:

> Thomas H. Davenport (1993), *Process Innovation: Reengineering Work through Information Technology*, Harvard Business School Press, Boston, Massachusetts.

For a detailed explanation of the difference between value-adding time and value-receiving time as well as an excellent discussion on the difference between density and speed in value transmission, please see:

Takahiro Fujimoto (1999), *The Evolution of a Manufacturing System at Toyota*, Oxford University Press, Oxford.

This chapter is a development of a text published in:

Pär Åhlström (2010), 'Om processers betydelse för verksamhets-utveckling i världsklass' (The Role of Processes when Developing World-class Operations) in Pär Åhlström (Ed.), *Verksamhetsutveckling i Världsklass* (*Developing World-class Operations*), Studentlitteratur, Lund.

## Chapter 3

Mathematically minded readers may be interested in the following technical description of the laws that govern how processes work:

Wallace J. Hopp and Mark L. Spearman (2000), *Factory Physics: Foundations of Manufacturing Management*, Irwin/McGraw-Hill, Boston, Massachusetts.

For a classical introduction to the phenomenon of bottlenecks in processes, please refer to:

Eliyahu M. Goldratt and Jeff Cox (1986), *The Goal: A Process of On-going Improvement*, North River Press, Crotonon-Hudson, New York.

The original formulation of the relationship between varia-tion, resource efficiency, and throughput time can be found in Kingman (1966). For a more easily accessible treatment of the relationship, as well as how the strategy of the Spanish cloth-ing retailer Inditex, with its Zara brand, can be understood using the relationship, we recommend Ferdows et al. (2004):

Sir John Frank Charles Kingman (1966), 'On the Algebra of Queues', *Journal of Applied Probability*, Vol. 3, No. 2, pp. 285–326.

Kasra Ferdows, Michael A. Lewis and Jose A.D. Machuca (2004), 'Rapid-Fire Fulfilment', *Harvard Business Review*, Vol. 82, No. 11, pp. 104–110.

This chapter is a development of a text published in:

Pär Åhlström (2010), 'Om processers betydelse för verksamhetsutveckling i världsklass' (The Role of Processes when Developing World-class Operations) in Pär Åhlström (Ed.), *Verksamhetsutveckling i Världsklass* (*Developing World-class Operations*), Studentlitteratur, Lund.

## Chapter 4

What we describe in the chapter as being superfluous work is similar to what John Seddon calls 'failure demand', a phenomenon occurring in services. Failure demand is defined as 'demand caused by a failure to do something or do something right for the customer'. By using the term 'superfluous work', we want to highlight the nature of the work being put in, not the demand. For a full discussion of failure demand, see:

John Seddon (2005), *Freedom from Command and Control: Rethinking Management for Lean Service*, Productivity Press, New York.

For a classic treatment of the nature of the human brain and its limited ability to process information, please see:

George A. Miller (1956), 'The Magical Number Seven, Plus or Minus Two: Some Limits on Our Capacity for Processing Information', *Psychological Review*, Vol. 63, No. 2, pp. 81–97.

## Chapter 5

Although Toyota was not necessarily the first company to develop many of the practices used in flow production, it is the company that has become most associated with flow-efficient manufacturing. For an excellent historical account of some of the antecedents to flow production, please see:

> Frank G. Woollard and Bob Emiliani (2009), *Principles of Mass and Flow Production*, Center for Lean Business Management, Wethersfield, Connecticut.

The history of the Toyota Production System has intentionally been kept short. There are many detailed accounts of the history for those who are interested. For a description of the Toyota Production System, directly from the 'source', we strongly recommend Ohno (1988). We have also taken the definitions of the seven forms of waste from his book:

> Taiichi Ohno (1988), *Toyota Production System: Beyond Large-Scale Production*, Productivity Press, New York.

The following article presents a great historical account of the development of the Toyota Production System:

> Matthias Holweg (2007), 'The Genealogy of Lean Production', *Journal of Operations Management*, Vol. 25, No. 2, pp. 420–437.

For an excellent analysis of the evolution of the Toyota Production System, we warmly recommend:

> Takahiro Fujimoto (1999), *The Evolution of a Manufacturing System at Toyota*, Oxford University Press, Oxford.

This chapter is a development of a text published in:

> Niklas Modig (2010), 'Vad är lean?' (What is Lean?) in Pär Åhlström (Ed.), *Verksamhetsutveckling i Världsklass (Developing World-class Operations)*, Studentlitteratur, Lund.

## Chapter 6

This chapter only touches on a fraction of all the literature there is on lean and Toyota. The chapter makes references to the following, in the order they appear in the text:

Taiichi Ohno (1988), *Toyota Production System: Beyond Large-Scale Production*, Productivity Press, New York.

John Krafcik (1988), 'Triumph of the Lean Production System', *Sloan Management Review*, Vol. 30, pp. 41–52.

James P. Womack, Daniel T. Jones and Daniel Roos (1990), *The Machine that Changed the World*, Rawson Associates, New York.

James P. Womack and Daniel T. Jones (1996), *Lean Thinking: Banish Waste and Create Wealth in your Corporation*, Simon and Schuster, New York.

Takahiro Fujimoto (1999), *The Evolution of a Manufacturing System at Toyota*, Oxford University Press, Oxford.

Steven Spear and H. Kent Bowen (1999), 'Decoding the DNA of the Toyota Production System', *Harvard Business Review*, Vol. 77, No. 5, pp. 96–106.

Jeffrey K. Liker (2004), *The Toyota Way: 14 Management Principles from the World's Greatest Manufacturer*, McGraw Hill, New York.

The survey was conducted in November 2010 by Eric A. Forsman and Dan Spinelli Scala as part of their Master's thesis at the Stockholm School of Economics.

## Chapter 7

For a more detailed explanation of level of abstraction, falsifiability, utility, and other building blocks of theory development, please see the following articles:

Samuel B. Bacharach (1989), 'Organisational Theories: Some Criteria for Evaluation', *Academy of Management Review*, Vol. 14, No. 4, pp. 496–515.

Chimezie A. B. Osigweh, Yg. (1989), 'Concept Fallibility in Organizational Science', *Academy of Management Review*, Vol. 14, No. 4, pp. 579–594.

David A. Whetten (1989), 'What Constitutes a Theoretical Contribution?' *Academy of Management Review*, Vol. 14, No. 4, pp. 490–495.

This chapter is a development of a text published in:

Niklas Modig (2010), 'Vad är lean?' (What is Lean?) in Pär Åhlström (Ed.), *Verksamhetsutveckling i Världsklass (Developing World-class Operations)*, Studentlitteratur, Lund.

## Chapter 8

For an easily accessible discussion of business strategies and the choices that companies face, please see:

Michael E. Porter (1980), *Competitive Strategy*, Free Press, New York.

Michael E. Porter (1996), 'What is Strategy?', *Harvard Business Review*, Vol. 74, No. 6, pp. 61–78.

To gain a better understanding of operations strategies, please see:

Nigel Slack and Michael Lewis (2011), *Operations Strategy*, Prentice Hall, London.

This chapter is a development of a text published in:

Niklas Modig (2010), 'Vad är lean?' (What is Lean?) in Pär Åhlström (Ed.), *Verksamhetsutveckling i Världsklass (Developing World-class Operations)*, Studentlitteratur, Lund.

## Chapter 9

All data regarding Toyota Motor Corporation and the Toyota car dealer network were collected by Niklas Modig between April 2006 and March 2008 within the scope of a larger research programme at the Manufacturing Management Research Center at the University of Tokyo.

For an explanation of Toyota Sales Logistics (in Japanese), see http://toyota.jp/after_service/syaken/sonoba/index.html (accessed on August 1, 2012).

## Chapter 10

All data regarding Toyota Motor Corporation and the Toyota car dealer network were collected by Niklas Modig between April 2006 and Match 2008 within the scope of a larger research program at the Manufacturing Management Research Center at the University of Tokyo.

Nishida-san is a made-up character, but the content of the story (explanations, illustrations, metaphors, etc.) comes from numerous interviews, discussions, and informal chats that Niklas Modig had with managers and employees from Toyota Motor Corporations and various Toyota car dealerships in Japan.

This chapter is a development of a text published in:

Niklas Modig (2010), 'Vad är lean?' (What is Lean?) in Pär Åhlström (Ed.), *Verksamhetsutveckling i Världsklass (Developing World-class Operations)*, Studentlitteratur, Lund.

## Chapter 11

The story about Ooba-san is most probably true, even if it has become an urban legend. One of the authors was told the story by Professor Jeffrey K. Liker at a conference in Sweden in November 2010.

This chapter is a development of a text published in:

Niklas Modig (2010), 'Vad är lean?' (What is Lean?) in Pär Åhlström (Ed.), *Verksamhetsutveckling i Världsklass (Developing World-class Operations)*, Studentlitteratur, Lund.